Notes of a
HALF-ASPENITE

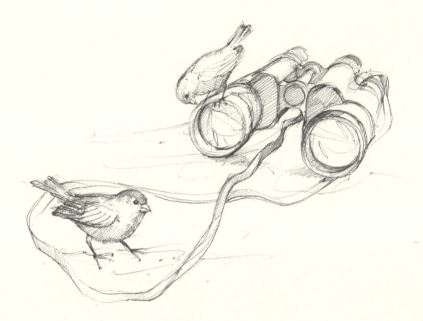

by Bruce Berger

Illustrations by Lynlie Hermann

Published by Ashley & Associates, Inc.

Illustrations by Lynlie Hermann
Design and Composition/Graphic Impressions, Inc.

© Copyright 1987, Bruce Berger
Library of Congress Catalog Number: 87-081838
International Standard Book Number: 0-914628-19-4
Printed in the United States of America

Published by Ashley & Associates, Inc.

Contents

For the town of Aspen,
so rich in life's crucial ingredient:
surprise.

Foreword

The following pieces were written under ideal circumstances: for a dozen years the publisher of *Aspen Magazine* allowed me to write, uncurbed, on subjects of my choice. A series of editors let themselves be bullied — occasionally by the author's phony threats to quit — into leaving the copy alone. In return I tried not to stray from the topic announced in the magazine's title and, if possible, not to bore. With the first pieces down, and more on the way, I plotted a book on the installment plan, and cheerfully confessed once the publisher suggested gathering them under one cover.

But this book grew like coral, not like architecture, and there is no grand plan. There are no disquisitions on mining, skiing, or real estate. Those looking for a reasoned history of Aspen should keep looking, and those who begin with the last page to see how the plot comes out find here a book they can't ruin. Whenever possible these articles modulate into essays, which is to say that facts drop away so that the author can flog his ideas. There is no conscious fabrication, but these pieces were written over time and the truth does not always stay put. Nor is time always sequence. If there is unity to these units, it comes from a town refracted through one sensibility — a sensibility numb to sports and economics, and gluttonous for the arts, birds, eccentrics, lunch, pratfalls, junk, and certain eccentricities of style.

Special and singular thanks must go to Su Lum, who held her detective's loupe to each piece as it was written and found the loose thread, the unlikely alibi, the hole in the evidence that would have fingered the author in print. If I was to suffer little tampering in the editorial room, it was because each piece arrived pre-sifted by Su, and I have her integrity to thank for preserving my own.

It is not often that a writer can remain with a publication for a dozen years, under a half-dozen changes of editorship, in collaboration that includes affection. Editors who have made that possible have been Rosemary Thompson, Virginia Hopkins, Nancy Kurtz, Randy Bernard, and, for two stints, Susan Michael. I am more than doubly indebted to Susan, who had the further patience to put up with the unglamorous mechanics of seeing this book into print. Such vitality and perseverance are a reflection of the publisher, Ernie Ashley, benign ringmaster, who has always granted full autonomy to her editors, reckless latitude to this writer, never failed in her support, and has proven that a magazine about Aspen can look beyond ballooning and deep powder to a town's full spectrum.

Gratitude is expressed to *Americana* for permission to reprint a piece on the Wheeler Opera House that appeared in its pages in slightly different guise. And ultimate gratitude goes to the town of Aspen, whose existence allows this book to be shelved in nonfiction.

Bruce Berger

Introduction

In the nearly quarter of a century that I have been coming to Aspen I have found myself asking — often — the following question: Is it possible to find happiness in a racially harmonious community, located in a beautiful valley, surrounded by high mountains, full of wonderful restaurants, superb skiing in the winter and superb music in the summer? My answer is yes — provided one has something else to do. I have always had something else to do — physics and writing — and so has Bruce, and this delightful, sometimes moving, always elegant book is a result. I have, incidentally, never thought that he bore the slightest resemblance to John Denver — see "The Face Is Familiar." Bruce is Bruce — blond, straw hat bearing, ready to laugh. As these essays show, he has — as those of us who know him know — a gift for friendship; or, perhaps better, a large tolerance for the human condition: something which, these days, takes a good deal of courage.

One of the pleasures of the book, at least for me, was the shock of recognition. I thought *I* was the only one who had defined an Aspen "local" as someone who was incapable of giving directions in terms of actual place names — see "Is Aspen Real?" I, like Bruce, am incapable of distinguishing among the streets Hopkins, Hyman and Hallam. The local apparently has other distinctions. The first night I got here, in June of 1963, I went in search of diversion and thought I had found it in a subterranean bar — long vanished — called the Pub, which I later learned was frequented by locals. I ordered a cognac, but before it appeared, a body — live — was slid forcefully from one end of the bar to the other at high velocity. My neighbor watched me as I watched this unexpected apparition and said, with uncanny accuracy, "You must be from the East." She, needless to say, was from Connecticut. If the Pub were still there and if I encountered a newly minted version of myself, as I was then, I am sure I would say, "You must be from the East."

Bruce, as the reader of these essays will learn, is not from the East, exactly, but from Chicago, having first arrived in Aspen at the age of 13 in 1952. The only two people I know personally who came here from the East earlier are Mortimer Adler and my former graduate school roommate, John Franklin Noxon III. I am not sure about Mortimer's first domicile, but Noxon's was a long and wide piece of unoccupied concrete piping, probably later used as a sewer. This unconventional housing was waterproof, conveniently shielded from the wind and, as it happened, very close to the ski slopes. After getting over the absurd notion that money should not be spent, Bruce informs us that he used his to buy the log-cabin style house which he still occupies. This house has, over the years, seen the likes of Tom Wolfe, Joyce Carol Oates and the memorable dog described in the essay "Og's End." This house has been, in Yeats's phrase, both "the dancer and the dance" — both a thing to be observed and a thing to observe from. Like the lovely essays in this book, it is a place of lights and shadows and unexpected sights, smells and sounds.

Jeremy Bernstein
Aspen, Colorado
July 17, 1987

1.

Landscapes Within

It is a tribute to the human interior how little it takes in the physical world to transform one's memories, associations, and attitudes, all the constellated feelings which are the core of one's relationship to a place. Although Aspen has altered radically over the years, in ways generally perceived for the worse, there is no way it can have changed in fact the way it has changed as myth in the minds of its loyal citizens, expatriates, converts, detractors, and true believers. The effort to chart one's relationship with a community in flux is rewarding if only as a guide to fresh landscapes within.

I first saw Aspen at the age of 13, primed as if for a religious conversion. I grew up, like many Aspenites, in suburban Chicago where summer was rich with insomnia and the elm leaves sticky with DDT, autumn was ruined by compulsory football practice, and winter was an endless tunnel of wind that ultimately burst, bright with forsythia, into baseball season. I always felt I belonged somewhere else, and would escape home after school, often through back alleys at a dead run, to lose my life in the family Steinway — or to dream of the mountains. Soon after I learned numbers I knew the precise heights of Mt. Elbert, Mt. Whitney, the Grand Teton, Popocatepetl, Aconcagua, Kilimanjaro, K2, and Everest. Their shapes were as familiar as our spaniel's ears, and from *National Geographic* I knew the lakes that lay between them — Victoria, Titicaca, Moraine Lake in the Valley of the Ten Peaks — a litany occasionally made tangible by an actual postcard.

Nor were my dreams entirely frustrated. My father was a retired accountant, increasingly plagued with asthma, and for the sake of his health we would take off for two months every winter to some scenic southern locale. My father's asthma was seldom alleviated but we basked in the fringe benefits of two winters in Florida, two in Arizona, one in Hawaii, one in Jamaica, one in Colorado Springs. My father tried new cures, my mother painted, and I became the scourge of hotel gin rummy tournaments. Class, when I returned, was still mired

1

in direct objects or long division, and meanwhile I was seeing the world.

When I reached high school my parents decided, perhaps correctly, that casual disappearances were no longer feasible, and sacrificed their annual escape for my future. But all was not lost. My half-sister, a generation older, had gone to Aspen on a brief ski vacation, had undergone some strange conversion, and was spending a winter there to see if it would do for the balance of her life.

When my first high school spring vacation arrived I boarded a train toward Aspen. I had picked up a few rudiments of skiing at a place called Wilmot, just over the Wisconsin border from Chicago, where a consumptive rope tow jerked one up someone's cow pasture for three turns back down through whitened manure. Wilmot has since graduated to chairlifts and pink snow, but Aspen was then a revelation. Ski classes obliged everyone to make it down the mountain by nightfall, but overtones of forced athletics were scant sacrifice for the rush of snow under one's feet, the exhilaration of becoming one's own vehicle.

Skiing, however, was merely a stalking horse for a far more insidious vice, which was Aspen. Aspen in 1952 was less a town than a conspiracy, or so it seemed to a suburban teen. One gloated to be there. The same sly faces repeated on the streets, in the bars (children were allowed if they would pretend not to drink), in liftlines, on the slopes and at the only two bistros. A floor show was improvised at the Golden Horn by ski instructors and jazz was improvised in the Red Onion by subversives like Dean Billings, Walt Smith, and Freddie Fisher. There was the lady who stood on her head on the piano. There was the doctor who set bones by day and felled billboards by night. There was Ralph Jackson, skiing in top hat, tails, and red underwear. Pins were given to skiers: one bell for surviving the mountain, two bells for stem turns, three bells for parallel, four bells for being a local superstar. The mountain, of course, was Ajax. There was a St. Bernard named Mambo who was a semi-official member of ski school. And hovering over all with a Swiss drawl and a slow sarcastic smile was Fred Iselin, Emperor of Ski School, whose photographs in sweater and stocking cap, arms folded and looking fierce, materialized around town with the caption, "Big Brother Is Watching You."

Such Easters were fairly corrupting to a young highschooler, but summer was worse. It became my duty to hike every trail, to clamber every mountain that did not demand ropes, and my secret mythology of lakes, once fairly catholic, was narrowed to the Elk Mountain

Range: Crater, Snowmass, Capitol. . . . Deprived of a Jeep trip, I could still turn out a fine pre-adolescent tantrum. And the Music Festival was the coup de grace: no rock and roll, no jazz, just week after week of the real thing.

Aspen on ten-day samplers was infused with a kind of glory. Nine spring vacations in a row I visited my sister, who had conveniently built a home and married the builder. There were seventeen trips by California Zephyr between Chicago and Glenwood Springs, each one a taste of freedom. I made friends with salesmen and retired train engineers, and once the Zephyr was packed with little old ladies on their way to the Coronation of Queen Elizabeth II. To a child previously exposed only to friends of parents, classmates, and the entrants of better gin rummy tournaments, Aspen was living democracy. And sensed less clearly but more profoundly, Aspen was another attitude toward life. Aspen did not seem based on competition. The schools I had known, with their exams and aggressive athletic programs, seemed to lead straight to the world of accountants, a waste of frustration and loneliness where the word *client* bonged like a call to battle. Aspen was the antithesis, a community collaborating to have fun. Aspen went on smoothly without me. But just as some children in the bewilderment of puberty turn to Pentecostal religions, hockey, model railroads, Demolay or crime, I converted to Aspen.

Remembered from Chicago, from schools in the East, charged with new values, vested with childhood mythology, Aspen shimmered like Byzantium. Locals, shopkeepers, the lucky few who had been born there, even long-term visitors, took on a sheen like demigods. I couldn't wait for gossip and my sister was right at the source. Secretary to the Chamber of Commerce, writing travel articles for national publication, assisting strangers, helping Aspen thrive, she held a position of significance and glamor (which she later reckoned paid five cents an hour), and her kinship was something to boast of during Aspen's first glow. What happened outside Aspen was a shadow play to be endured.

But I never considered adulthood in Aspen. I had ruled out becoming an accountant, the one future half-tamed by proximity, and the best dodge seemed to be academia. A certain boredom still clung, but the university was self-enclosed, valued literature, prolonged the bull session, shielded one from the empty wars of business, and offered one friends, sustenance and community. Best of all, the ascent to the Ph.D. prolonged school itself another three years, postponing self-reliance. After finishing college on the East Coast I repaired to graduate school on the West Coast, pausing only briefly in Aspen. But college was no longer the same. Graduate classes were larger, duller, more anonymous, and merely required more work. I never felt so alone. One night in the Berkeley library, debating whether to read four centuries of literary criticism on *The Winter's Tale* chronologically to understand it, or alphabetically to keep track of it, illumination struck: *school was interfering with my education.* I chucked all the books down the chute and ended, with lasting relief, my academic career.

I did not, however, take off for Aspen, but for Cannery Row in Monterey, where I had already taken up on weekends with artists opening a framing studio. My father had died during my senior year of college, leaving me enough money to live on, but it seemed irresponsible to use it. The family ethic held that a man was to leave money to his children, but his children were to squirrel it away for emergencies and begin a fresh round of sacrifice for the next generation. Meanwhile the vaguely Marxist values I had picked up since leaving the nest, from across an ethical chasm, equally belittled coupon-clipping. "The conscience of the rich" is one of those phrases which is intrinsically funny, and is nonetheless real. But put a non-competitive person in a competitive society, give him some alternative to working, and he will find a way around his conscience. . . .

On Cannery Row I knocked out frames, drank, and scribbled poetry. The image of Aspen sometimes overcame me and I would return, alone or with friends, intending to stay three weeks, and spend five months. I rented cabins. I lingered long enough to look down on tourists. I took off for Europe, accidentally found work in Spain, and stayed three years. I flew to New York for a family wedding, promised my Spanish friends a speedy return, and wound up back in Aspen. The place was making me a liar. I settled into the Floradora, providing guest taxi service in return for a room deduction. Suddenly my sister got first right of refusal on the house next door to her. It was an Early Fritz Benedict cabin of logs from the Midnight Mill, perched at the end of Main Street on an acre of land over Castle Creek, with a cottonwood grove toward town and an opposing panorama from Shadow Mountain through Highlands to Willow Valley. Did I want it? I put my immoral dividends to work.

The luxury of a house in Aspen at first so overwhelmed me that I felt guilty, wrong about owning it. The man who had previously rented it expected his own first option to buy and was crushed. I kept running into him. How had I deserved it? Guiltily, I rearranged it, filled it with junk redeemed from garage sales, turned out manu-

scripts in my chosen corner, filled its emptiness with my life. Principles vanished, I watched the seasons turn, made a few repairs, and it became mine.

Meanwhile, beyond my drive, in greater nirvana, the pace was quickening. Buildings were rising, traffic was thickening, prices were spiraling. One saw more strangers than friends on the street: the efforts of my sister and her fellow converts were succeeding all too well. And what were Aspen's cheerful conspirators doing now? Some, like Freddie Fisher, had died; some had moved on in disgust; some had gone into hiding; some, like my sister, turned to volunteer work for health and service organizations. But there were many locals, oldtimers, and colorful merchants, it now appeared, who did not care to salvage the old Aspen. They wanted it glossier, more lucrative. Behind the funny hats and clever Winterskol floats they were propelled by the deadly old values, and Aspen was their medium.

A coalition of old guard and acquisitive newcomers dominated City Council and the County Commission, and they did not see the problem because to a large measure they *were* the problem. The unacquisitive young were construed as a threat. Resentments crystallized in an immigrant restaurateur who became City Magistrate, who openly boasted of punishments he was going to inflict for blocking the sidewalk and disturbing the peace on defendants whose cases he had not heard, but whose abundant hair and scruffy clothes had already proven them morally offensive and bad for business. The American Civil Liberties Union formed in Aspen for the stated purpose of relieving said magistrate and ultimately succeeded, but meanwhile the town lived in a mentality of civil war. Perhaps Aspen was swept up in larger tides, perhaps I was merely discovering the view through the cottonwoods, but paradise up close seemed half snakes.

Aspen's schizophrenia climaxed with Hunter Thompson's now-legendary race for sheriff, when the lives of both candidates were threatened, the BBC swooped in with the eyes of the world and the pitch of hysteria resulted in such a narrow defeat of the no-growth insurgents that in subsequent, calmer elections they prevailed. The business hegemony was broken. What tipped the balance was the influx of newcomers who did not want to make money or had already made it. They saw Aspen headed for the very nightmares they were trying to escape, knew exactly what Aspen had to lose, and were trying to save it from the latest corporate seductions. Political feelings cooled, as they had to, and have since resulted in some consensus about Aspen's future, even as Aspen becomes a pleasure capital for the media. Aspen is still threatened by counterrevolution for profit, still defended by a vigilant core determined to preserve the old village and its free land, but as Aspen fattens on peaceful times, its tensions recede farther from the surface.

Aspen, on binges of introspection, too often defines itself in isolation, as if creation ended on its jagged horizon, or as if its problems would vanish if only the outside world would leave it alone. But Aspen is a mere point on a long historical curve that began centuries back in Europe when the dissatisfied fled a continent where one lived where one's parents lived, took over their jobs, fought their wars, worshipped their gods. In migrating to America many of the ancient restrictions were dropped, and others inadvertently lost as the hopeful invaded a fresh continent, created new towns, homesteaded, colonized plains and valleys, leveled forests, displaced a race unable to fight back, and were unbridled by the very wilderness they sought to civilize. The restlessness of the European immigrant, his demand for self-fulfillment, his material and emotional quest is a trajectory that leads directly to Aspen. A few have made the leap in a single lifetime. And Aspen, for all its cultural and architectural overtones of Europe, is uniquely American. What has now become the rage of self-realization, abetted by encounter groups, Eastern religions, and mass psychological catharses, all that is summed up with sad utility by the phrase, contemporary lifestyle — what Tom Wolfe referred to as the Me-Decade — has reached its logical destination in this free-living valley. Having survived its Oedipal crisis with the Hunter Thompson election, Aspen has thrown off parental repression to enter a time of tolerance, money, pleasure, self-gratification and even, for those willing to turn an occasional back on its enticements, a measure of creativity.

It is a popular cliche that Aspen, because of its shortage of muggings, rapes, racial tensions, busing fights and Ramada Inns, is not real. The dark side of hedonism, its masochistic snag in the wake of political assassinations, Vietnam and Watergate, holds that only the ugly is real. It is nonetheless a philosophical verity that everything that exists is real. Even Aspen is real. If Aspen has managed to evade many of the plagues of contemporary America even by accident of wealth and isolation, it remains a human possibility, a useful example for good as well as for ill. The populace of Aspen, along with its insularity and excess, appreciates human variety in an unspoiled setting. It remains alert, enthusiastic, well-informed. The reality of Aspen, like the conscience of the rich, may be unlikely, but it is not fictitious.

Yet having owned up to the perfect residence in this largely idyllic town, with time and the means to indulge, the rest must be confessed: the mythology is gone. Partly, of course, one simply cannot sustain the Olympus of one's teens. No matter how one resists, one grows up. A parallel factor is the change in Aspen itself — yet much of that change has been for the better. Along with condominiums, traffic, expense, publicity, a rising crime rate and the disappearance of singular oldtimers, there is by force of numbers a greater human spectrum. There is perhaps the richest concentration of good eating in America, an ambitious literary magazine, decent movies, winter concerts, serious year-around theater, three blocks for pedestrians, fine visual arts, and even recycling: Aspen is no longer the one-dimensional pleasure capital to which culture was applied, like a poultice, for two months every construction season. But balance that against an ironic family of Americans and Europeans who took over a Victorian enclave with potholes, vacant lots, horse trails in every direction, a visit from Schweitzer, a Skier of the Week named Frissy Titsworth, old boilers, overgrown trails, a downtown elk and indolence for the scandal of your choice. Superimpose a history of infighting, congestion, diesel smog, tabloid violence, the desertion of earlier converts and the simultaneous convergence of all one's loved ones on one's lodgings, and it is no longer possible to believe that Aspen, the sampled apple, is paradise regained.

My own case contains one extraneous element. In October of 1963 I took a trip through the Glen Canyon in Utah, just prior to its annihilation by Glen Canyon Dam. Utah slickrock reawakened for me the presence of the desert, first experienced in 1947 during our first family winter in Arizona: a landscape where each element stands revealed, each rock with its shadow, each plant in its compass of available water. Doves, quail, flickers, jackrabbits, coyotes, hawks, and lizards all bristle like strands of contemporary music among cactus, palo verdes, ironwood and mesquite — a cackling ecosystem that seems, in retrospect, to have been waiting patiently beyond the mountains of childhood. Since that trip through the Glen, I have come to haunt Southeast Utah, Southern Arizona, and the Baja Peninsula; just as taste in color can change from early purple through deep blue and red, to settle somewhere among the rusts and siennas, so has a longing for space shifted from this abrupt drama of the mountains to the far earth tones and barbed shadows of the desert. Aspen, too ingrained to abandon, has become a house, friends, ongoing traditions, committees, sprawling bookshelves, a place to order the manuscripts and memories of somewhere else.

Since rediscovering the desert I have been shadowed by an image composed of a number of places seen and reimagined. A stand of cottonwoods darkens an outcropping of water, perhaps flowing a few yards, perhaps only touching roots. To the horizon in all directions stretches rock or sand or waste. Footprints, smooth, webbed or clawed, trail to that vortex of desolation as if to a hand half gone from squeezing the sky. A few birds are phrasing the silence. It is to its inhabitants the focus of known life, isolated, vulnerable, irreplaceable, and that is all. It has, I suspect, more meanings than I have teased out, but the place pursues me like a waking dream, a mandala, a landscape of the heart.

I now divide my time between Phoenix and Aspen. Phoenix is one of the newest and rawest cities in the world. My mother has a spread in the subdivided desert where I can write, and friends in the rotting core are tolerant when I let off steam. Downtown Phoenix is particularly corrective because Aspen, aggressively real, is nonetheless out of touch with the American mainstream. Phoenix is not. Ambulances wail all night. Gordon's Market, under a decaying plaster chicken, has a clientele which is unglamorous regardless of race, color or national origin, trying to find enough bargains to make it through tomorrow. At the neighborhood bar, there is a man with a disability pension from a nerve gas experiment whose joy is to commit a sex act daily with a member of the opposite race, a woman who devotes her life to Coors and her twelve cats, a veteran of the original cast of *Oklahoma*, a black proofreader with a taste for martinis and self-defense, and an unemployment investigator who is writing a musical comedy about the Lost Dutchman Mine. You might not encounter them at the Paragon, but they are worth knowing. And past downtown Phoenix and suburbia, past tracts and smog and citrus groves, is still pure desert.

Long winters in Aspen I become that boring villain, the absentee landlord. Yet Aspen, like Hemingway's Paris, is not so easy to shake. Unless you lie about your residence you are assaulted with John Denver and Hunter Thompson. When the Claudine affair broke, Main Street Haircutting in Scottsdale called for the inside scoop. *Aspen,* the novel, was plugged for weeks between movie ads in the Phoenix dailies and racked by the cash registers of supermarkets. Aspen the Dodge nearly runs you down. The Aspen courthouse appeared almost nightly on CBS news. If you are in Phoenix to forget Aspen, forget it.

Before I left Arizona last year, when daytime temperatures eased off around 107 degrees and summer was still coming, I went into the desert just to see what would happen. I had expected a welcome of insects, lizards, snakes, scorpions, and chuckawallas, all the cold-blooded predators warmed for action, but the cactus lay stunned in silence, an expanse of broken statuary through which I seemed the only moving thing. Sweat ran salt in my eyes. My thirst became pathological. When I returned home I chugged two beers nearly nonstop before I could explain myself. But did I dream of my childhood mountains? No. Conversely, in my study this summer I heard a soft skreak like a rusty pump, and crept around to investigate. Perched on the scrub oak just outside, a foot from the glass, was the red-tailed hawk who ranges just below Shadow Mountain, whom I had despaired of seeing up close and who had recently been displaced as chief bird by the evening hang gliders. I must have been obscured by bright reflections, for he shifted his talons anxiously on the branch and twisted his square head in quick observant jerks over his breast of pale salmon, yet never started as I crept forward until we were nearly beak to nose. When he finally burst through the leaves, all I could think of was to get back to the desert.

Recently in the Superstition Mountains, about which my friend will write his musical, I wandered away from companions just before sundown to watch the last light over the confluence of two drainages. One tributary stirred faintly with water, the other was dry. A few Fremont cottonwoods took the air with a muted rustling. A phainopepla, the black cardinal, repeated a few times its one reedy question. Light sank, weeds and mallow nodded in a late updraft, and beyond the small oasis the cactus stood at attention like creatures awaiting their first breath. For a few minutes there was no distinction between movement and sound. There was only the single but collective presence of the place, the focus of life, that seemed to meet some stilled attention within. The sensation lasted only a few moments, and rates comparatively low in the hierarchy of states. But it is one I have not experienced in the Roaring Fork Valley.

2.

Snow on the Cultural Desert

Walter Paepcke may have envisioned Aspen as a new start for the whole man, but the end of August has traditionally meant a last concert, a parting lecture, the demise of art classes, dance camps, writing workshops, theater projects, pottery groups, sculpting, photography, collage and transcendence: a farewell to the mind and resumption of the body. There have always been those who have resented the split itself, and particularly the defeat of their favorite side by five to one, and being among them I enlisted in the Winter Concert Committee of 1969. I had little idea what adventure lay out in the snow.

My first assignment seemed elementary: to collect from the Glenwood Springs station a highly praised former piano student of the Aspen Music School named Etsuko Tazaki, selected from the pool of talent at our disposal through Young Artists of Aspen. I arrived well ahead of the afternoon train and was informed it would be a little late. I was armed with a book, finished the last chapter, bought another. As the afternoon wore on and literature paled I pressed the stationmaster for details. No need to worry, he assured me, the train was only a few miles up the canyon and temporarily stalled, it seemed, because a flat car from another train was askew on the track. I decided to drive up the canyon for a look.

The train was grounded three miles upstream. I hadn't appreciated that at any point the canyon was so wide; immediately below lay the Colorado River, spanned by a footbridge, beyond which stretched a field of unbroken snow walled on the far side by a freight train and the California Zephyr. I parked, leaving the lights on because the shoulder was narrow and dusk thickening, and tried the bridge. It was amply wide and swung cheerfully over the snarling water, giving a queasy sensation midway where the cable swooped almost to the planking. I was welcomed on the far side by two barking dogs.

The field lay frozen beneath eighteen-inch drifts, through which I plodded to the Zephyr's engine. The engineer leaned out and asked

11

my business. He seemed unsurprised by the answer and cautioned me to stay on the river side of the train. From the road the Zephyr had sparkled like a Lionel, but up close it multiplied itself car by car into a steel fortress as I craned for a Japanese face and prowled for a way to get in. The stair between the last sleeper and the observation was down, and I hopped aboard.

I entered the observation car and became the immediate center of alarmed attention. "Have you been out in the snow?" "Are you going to make a run for it?" Suddenly aware of my dripping parka and boots, I retreated to the vestibule, shook and stamped, then started forward with coat and mitts in hand.

I peered into all open roomettes, scanned the club car and diner, pushed through the coaches where hundreds of college students were getting drunk, reached the end and started back, this time checking all the vista domes. I reached the observation car more anonymously this time and started back on my third lap. In the diner I asked the steward if I could have someone paged. "I'm too busy," he snapped, announced third call to dinner and resumed his gossip with the waiters. I continued forward and noticed that in the third coach a green overcoat had slipped from a sleeping form to reveal an Eastern face. "Etsuko?" I asked. "EtSUko?"

The eyes opened sleepily. "Yes," she answered, "Etsko," correcting my pronunciation.

I sat down and explained my mission. She came awake and laughed. It was too late to play, the college students were so noisy, it was so pleasant to sleep. . . .

Sorry, I said, but there was still ample time if we could make it from the train to the road with the luggage. Fine, but for one detail, she said: her only shoes were the high heels she had on, and they would never make it through eighteen inches of snow.

For half an hour we laughed over imagined solutions. We could ask some Aspen-bound skier to lend us a pair of boots long enough to get to a concert . . . . no, no one was *that* drunk. Suddenly the train started backward and I thought we were headed to Denver. It stopped after a hundred feet.

I had read once of derelicts wrapping their feet with newspapers to keep warm, and suggested to Etsuko that perhaps boots could be devised that would last to the road. She seemed unimpressed but agreed to a prowl through the train for inspiration.

We started back like a pair of magpies, scouring all vacant seats for remnants. While sacking a roomette we became aware of a porter watching us quietly across the aisle, and pressed on. We turned up two windfalls: a complete *Chicago Sunday Tribune* and one foot-sized plastic bag. On the way back through the club car we cadged string from the bartender.

We returned to Etsuko's seat for some quick cobbling. My boots fit her without quite falling off, and newspapers bound with string around my ankles and stuffed on one side into the plastic bag survived a much stared-at test run down the aisle. I dismantled them and we headed to the baggage compartment at the end of the car.

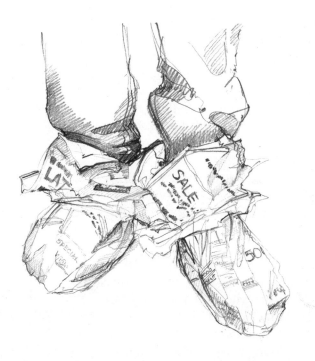

Etsuko's fat canvas lay near the bottom. We wrestled the top ones down and were just getting close when the porter arrived. Explaining we needed something inside, we grabbed Etsuko's bag and headed through the vestibule. Through coaches, diner, club car and room-ettes we barged our way, Etsuko with my parka and gloves, news-paper, plastic bag and string, I with her stuffed canvas. Expecting to be detained as potential train robbers, whenever we encountered a figure in uniform we returned the look that impelled Ralph Ellison to write *Invisible Man*. Passengers asked whether we planned to get off; we advanced in silence. We passed the conductor once too often, this time with luggage. "Where are you two headed?" We doubled our speed. "Where are you going?"

It was a desperate ploy, but our only hope. We told him the truth.

"Fine. I'll let you off several cars ahead so you won't have to walk so far through the snow." We stared almost in disappointment: not even surprise. No worry, I thought, wait till he sees the newspaper trick.

With the conductor in the lead we staggered back through the roomettes, the club car, the diner, the coaches. Comments were now in the open: Them again! Conductor caught them headed to the roomettes. I knew those two were up to no good. Game's up now . . .

We reached the last vestibule and the conductor lowered the stair. I mumbled something about boots and started binding my feet in the *Chicago Tribune*; the conductor stared glassily as if caught by one more dreary late show. We thanked him profusely and started down. "Good luck," he muttered, and was gone before we reached the snow.

As we started along the train the newspaper felt warm and secure. The moon was nearly full, shadowing my broken track across the field, and the canyon shimmered like a trough of blue glass. The snow felt light and dry.

As we started across my feet quickly chilled, particularly my right, lacking its plastic bag. I looked down; the bottom had gone through to the sock. Etsuko forged behind without comment. The field seemed newly huge. Then dogs started barking; we were nearly across. My feet were now evenly congealed, the left having littered its plastic, and I shifted Etsuko's penitential canvas.

I lurched heavily onto the footbridge with a brain full of frostbite. Etsuko, whose two familiar landscapes were Tokyo and New York, found herself swinging wildly between two cables over the Colorado River, but was too horrified to comment until later. We scrambled triumphantly up the far bank to my car, which still had its lights on.

All this for a dead battery? But the motor turned with a flick of the key, the heater warmed, I peeled my socks and cradled my feet in my hands and Etsuko poured snow from my boots. It was 7:20, slightly over an hour until performance.

From Glenwood Springs I called Betty Feinsinger, Etsuko's hostess, to confirm our approach, and we arrived in Aspen on the stroke of 8:30. I dropped Etsuko at the Feinsingers' to change, grab a bite and thaw her fingers on their piano, then rushed to Paepcke Auditorium with the good news. Edgar Stanton, a committee member who heard the story in the lobby, held the audience by passing it on with a few flourishes, and Etsuko entered at 9:15 to sustained applause. Sailing through a Bach Prelude and Fugue, the

Schumann G Minor Sonata and the Beethoven *Diabelli Variations*, she received a standing ovation. Yet even the heroic concert with post mortems we never could have invented was too little to see music through an Aspen winter, for the two-thirds attendance at her concert dropped to a few rows for the next, and we were forced to cancel the remainder of the series.

Etsuko Tazaki has gone on to solo with symphonies in the United States and Japan, the pianist who braved our second concert was later discovered by a committee member to have reached Bora Bora as a Mormon missionary, and winter concerts have become reliable events. Summer still lends a now-or-never panic to the lecture, master class, or concert, lest in mid-February the stored heat run out and the right hand twitch toward Johnny Carson. But besides bars, churches, and voting booths, Aspen can now anticipate year-around theater, psychic encounter, Asiatic self-defense, domestic salvation, extension courses, performance workshops, poetry read-ings, gallery openings, historic zoning, and people quietly being themselves. And the more Aspen's creative life consolidates, the more it may need, to hold its edge, the grace of something gone wrong.

3.

Notes of A Half-Aspenite

They say there are no two snowflakes alike, but I've found they vary less than, say, saguaro cactus. Perhaps the ski monoculture was getting to me, for after sufficient winters of enduring a layer of dead white between myself and the Aspen I most admire, I joined the retirement set and started fleeing to Arizona. The price in esteem is steep. Residents at both ends gush that you have the best of both worlds, their voices edged enough to imply, in Arizona, that you can't take the heat, and in Colorado that you can't take the cold. One becomes a turkey here, a snowbird there, and the ornithological insults never stop. Nevertheless, along about late October or early November, whenever the weather starts getting flaky, it is time to brave the asides, load up the Toyota, and head for the land of blue-hairs and rattlesnakes. I am, in the words of a friend's child, the Last of the Summer People.

But Phoenix is a tacky place. The Salt River Valley, once ringed by a surgically clean horizon, has been littered with hundreds of city blocks festering between Sun City, the original retirement rookery, and the gift shop ghetto of Scottsdale, a kind of tourist trots become architecture. The desert, which struck some inner chord when I first saw it as a second grader in 1946, is still home; but to get from the outpost where I scribble to human companionship downtown, I must blow monoxide for numberless miles each way. I think of it, in the language of smog reports, as my winter inversion.

And as I shrink in the minds of Aspenites to a villainous absentee landlord, the image of Aspen floats back like a pledge of deliverance. It is hardly nostalgia for the Rockies, less interesting than the rhyolite escarpments locally available. It is Aspen the tiny metropolis — intimate, unpredictable, bound by three bridges — that glimmers like a lost civilization. A plane ticket would only get me into snow. Time will eventually take me there by car, but the only immediate recourse is to leaf through my sporadic journals for those entries that release, at least to their keeper, the sting of summer dust. A few:

July 19, 1976
 More global villagers on the mall. Around seventy hooded Iranian students paraded the west end shouting "Death to the Shah!" and handing out leaflets denouncing political repression; on the east end a brass band was bouncing through Scott Joplin; and on a bench in between, ignoring all competitors, sat a couple of suburban kids strumming banjos and singing mountain songs as if born on a stoop in Kentucky.

August 14, 1978
 Sent Katie Lee a packet of manuscripts for criticism and decided to soften her up with a wildlife stamp of her favorite animal, a snake. The postman put the envelope on the scale, spotted the red racer looped like a pretzel, clapped his hands to his forehead, gave a guttural cry, and retreated through the packages. He returned looking a little bloodless, and tried to read the scale without looking at the envelope. "Forty-one cents," he said, "and thanks for ruining my day."

June 21, 1980
 Su Lum called in some distress: a week ago she had been taking a shower when she heard a rattling and shrieking just outside the house. She grabbed a robe and flung open the front door. A chipmunk that had been caught between the front and storm doors fled into the house, pursued by her several cats, disappeared behind the record cabinet, and hadn't been seen since. She had no idea whether it was still there, had somehow escaped, or had died, but she dropped a few bread crumbs behind the cabinet daily, just in case. Besides humane considerations, chipmunks and other small rodents were known carriers of bubonic fleas, and the city a few summers back had created a minor scandal by poisoning the gophers on the golf course. Bubonic fleas are as native to Colorado as columbine, are primarily dangerous when the carrier dies and the insect is looking for a new host, and City Councilman Steve Wishart offered a calmer solution when he suggested we give up playing with dead chipmunks. Yet here we were, faced with that very prospect.
 We banished Su's domestic animals, emptied the cabinet of its records, then contrived a small runway involving a desk and some album covers leading from the cabinet to the front door. There remained a small gap, which I intended to fend with a broom. Su pulled the cabinet forward. I braced for action. Nothing stirred. We peered behind the cabinet and discovered a small dead chipmunk.

Now came the most perilous moment: the removal of the chipmunk from the house without contracting the plague. We debated alternatives, then decided upon tongs and foil. I spread the foil on the floor, lifted the chipmunk onto the center with the tongs, folded the foil with the tongs around the deceased until it resembled a silver enchilada, then bore the ensemble at arm's length while Su opened, in turn, the back door, the gate, and the garbage can lid. We then boiled the tongs, washed our hands twice, and hoped the matter closed.

October 16, 1978
Lightning struck the TV relay antenna and we missed the special on "The Violent Universe."

August 21, 1977
Found an item buried in the *Aspen Times* Activities Calendar: "Sunday, 9:30 A.M., Opticon Theater, Snowmass, Margaret Mead speaking to the L-5 Society on space colonies." No other mention in the paper. Called Su Lum, who works for the *Times*. Would this be *the* Margaret Mead?

"Seems obscure to me too," said Su, "but the Activities Calendar is not my department. We'd better check it out."

It was eerie to walk into a movie theater at 9:25 on a Sunday morning, as if for some fringe religion. On stage was a large TV screen, and our hearts sank: we would probably see Professor Mead on videotape. Along with a few aspiring space migrants we sat for what seemed an age in the penumbra, feeling we'd lit on some way station that tried to simulate, not too successfully, conditions on earth. Who were these people who wanted to live in a distant bubble? They looked like your average movie crowd except for a fierce-looking elderly lady in a crimson cape, bearing a lacquered five-foot walking stick and striding like Columbus down the aisle. When she reached the lectern and tapped the mike I realized, with a shock, that I was staring at Margaret Mead.

"Can you all hear me?" she demanded. There was silence. "It would be just like Americans to sit there for an hour missing the lecture and then complain about it later. If anyone can't hear, I want to know *now*." Acoustics were not a problem.

She had spent her life studying island cultures, she told us, and space colonies were the ultimate island cultures. By studying the social dynamics of Samoa and New Guinea, we could learn what not to do in space. She had hoped to contribute her advanced age to the first floating society, but feared she had overdone it. . . .

I admired her wayfaring spirit, but less than the earthly surprise in Aspen's own planned satellite. What will our orbiting movie theaters do for exotic birds?

December 7, 1982

I called to ask how my renter enjoyed being back in Aspen.

"God," she sighed, "after my exile in Santa Fe, you can't imagine how I looked forward simply to the conversation. Books, music, art, travel — I couldn't wait. Since I've been back, I've been to a party almost every night. And do you know the only thing anyone talks about?" She paused as if loath to pronounce it. "Zoning."

August 1, 1975

Larry visiting from Denver. Couldn't decide between Scrabble at home or delirium at the Paragon, so we compromised with Scrabble at the Paragon. It seemed unchallenging to play amid Victorian furniture, so we headed to the disco side, grabbed two chairs and a cocktail table, ordered drinks, and unfolded the board. Music so loud we tallied by gesture. A crowd gathered; strangers screamed at us, wanted to know what we were doing, why we were doing it here, and insisted on pointing out words we were about to miss. Finally neither of us could play without a dozen collaborators who would rather spell than dance; the people here must be starved to use their verbal skills. Now understand Shakespeare's line about the paragon of animals. Conceded the game to delirium.

August 24, 1975
A middle-aged couple strolling ahead of me suddenly stopped by the health food store, struck by a poster of the well-known teenage guru, Nirvana Fats, smiling beatifically through a nimbus of stars. "Edith," the man cried, "that's the guy with the hangar next to ours!"

September 5, 1979
Was happily rejecting submissions at the Aspen Leaves office in the Opera House when I heard a nasty snarl from the mall. A bulldozer was hoisting a heap of dirt, surmounted by the granite pedestal with the heroic marble derrière for which the city paid a reported five thousand of our tax dollars. Neglected schemes flashed through my mind: the letter to the *Times* complaining that $5,000 was too much for a piece of ass, even in Aspen; the intention to apply a band-aid in the night. Relocation was still in progress when I crossed the mall with a handful of rejects and ran into my friend Pierre. "Look at that," he beamed. "Don't you just love to see the city haul ass?"

July 28, 1982
Was having lunch on the patio at Pinocchio's when out of the corner of my eye I saw a woman attaching something to the fence and commanding, "Stay!" I turned out to see what kind of dog it was. It was a Schwinn.

August 29, 1978
A sheriff's deputy appeared at the door with a paper to serve on an ex-renter's ex-girlfriend. Told her I was sorry but couldn't help. "While I'm here," she asked, "do you mind if I play an A on your piano? I'm trying to develop my pitch." She hummed, then struck a note. "Damn, always a half-tone flat. Anyway, thanks."

August 21, 1977
A month ago I found the stalls of the Hotel Jerome's men's room had been freshly painted white, so I scrawled "Béla Bartók bangs." Went back today and found the phrase amended fore and aft by a variety of hands, so that it now runs the length of the stall and reads, "Betcha Beleaguered Béla Bartók Bangs Boogie Baby But Bad."

August 19, 1972

Had a small meet-the-candidate evening for Congressional aspirant Alan Merson. A young man I hadn't met before showed up in a coat and tie — exotic dress for Aspen — and grilled Merson in a tone that implied reservoirs of political knowledge. At last he ducked into the bathroom, and apparently failed to turn on the light, for he emerged holding a can of Ajax I'd left on the hamper instead of his beer. He resumed his interrogation gesturing with the cleanser, and I was secretly annoyed with my fellow Democrat who pointed it out well before he raised it to his lips.

August 30, 1972

Su Lum's house guest had spent the day splicing and resplicing a fifty-foot reel of himself mastering the stem turn last March: would I be kind enough to enlarge the audience? A reminder of why I leave Aspen in the winter never hurts, so I agreed.

We dowsed the lights, and Vance turned on the projector. There on the screen was the projectionist, skiing upside down. The lights came back on, Vance reversed the reels. There was the projectionist on his feet, skiing uphill and backward. On with the lights while Vance rewound the reel and started over. There was the projectionist executing some fine stem turns while a dark undergrowth crept toward him from the margins of the screen. We peered into the projector, and found it full of cat and dog hairs that the film had collected during the splicing and dispersed during the screening. The reel couldn't last much longer; surely we could get through it. Vanced rolled it while Su ran the film through a brace of Q-tips before it entered the gears. Darkness bristled in. We stopped the machine, Su brought out the vacuum and attacked all sides with the hose. We ran the rest of the film and watched the remains of a skier being eaten by a time-lapse jungle. Never have I experienced a more satisfying winter.

February 23, 1982

Killed the afternoon watching Gila woodpeckers and rifling back journals for vignettes of Aspen. Must have been the prospect of Misha Dichter playing piano with the Phoenix Symphony in the evening. Most of the entries could have happened anywhere — but they don't. Survived the toxic drive downtown, reached the Civic Plaza marquee proclaiming "Monday and Tuesday — Phoenix Symphony Orchestra with Sisha Dicater." Am learning to read Phoenician. The usual Monday crowd: fur stoles, aggressive perfumes, intermission starring a grande dame in purple feathers, rumored to be the Wife of Kaibab Industries. But as Dichter played, I could close my eyes, block out the Chanel, and imagine his last Sunday morning rehearsal in Aspen when Su remarked that the open cello cases looked like a coffin display, Mekeel complained that the hardboiled egg she bought at the lemonade stand splattered yolk on her shift, and the conductor's dog had to be pried from the pedals. The clarity of the piano was nearly tactile. Wind whipped through the canvas with a breath of sage.

4.

Atoms In Eden

"There is the idea of a universe parallel to ours but moving in the opposite direction along the axis of time, whose interface with our own may be black holes," wrote a physicist to me recently in seemingly human scrawl. It has been known for some time that light is bent and time slowed by gravity, and that the farther an object is from us, the faster it is moving. A force few have heard of, the color force, holds our smallest constituents together, while entities called neutrinos rain continually through us, seldom encountering a lonely atom. Using borrowed energy, nature can create any kind of particle at any time as long as it simultaneously creates its anti-particle. And those particles are possessed not only of charge, mass and duration, but such exotica as upness, downness, charm, spin and strangeness, with the lurking possibility of truth and beauty. For the final stretcher, Steven Weinberg, a Harvard professor who has perpetrated much of this nonsense, has exclaimed that the universe may be simpler than it looks.

An Aspen visitor who is working to find out whether protons decay has said that just as the place for a physicist to be in the '20s was in Copenhagen around Niels Bohr, and in the late '40s was in Princeton around Einstein and Oppenheimer, the place to be now — at least in the summer — is Aspen. Every important contemporary physicist is said to have passed through town, over a dozen have taken up residence, and the Aspen Post Office has called the Aspen Center for Physics the largest summer business. Yet physicists seem to pass through Aspen like neutrinos, leaving little trace, and even the buildings are those cinderblocks of squared-off grey matter peculiar to Aspen Institute property, as if they took too literally the expression "think tank," or the notion of anti-charm.

But the history of the Aspen Center for Physics is anything but drab, starting with George Stranahan arriving here to ski in 1947, then spending summers here a decade later as relief from graduate school. He had contracted the Aspen virus, tried to do physics in a rented garage, couldn't concentrate, and thought it might help if there were more of his kind. In 1960 he met Bob Craig, then president of the Aspen Institute for Humanistic Studies, and proposed a physics center. Craig was interested and suggested that he talk it up among fellow physicists. George's professor in Pittsburgh put him in touch with a Michael Cohen at the University of Pennsylvania, who was talking about a summer camp for physicists that might be combined with mountaineering. Stranahan, Craig and Cohen met at the Pittsburgh Airport, and the Aspen Center for Physics was born.

Cohen, it turned out, wanted some sort of tent city, while George preferred something more formal, with a nonprofit corporation and a live building. The triumvirate came to an agreement and divided the labors: Cohen was to corral physicists and talk to the National Science Foundation, Craig was to line up the Institute, and Stranahan was to fund-raise and get the building built. George describes it as a kind of three-legged stool, any leg of which would function if the other two were already in place. The physicists were the easiest to convince, and the Institute came around when Stranahan, Craig and Robert O. Anderson met naked in a sauna. In the winter of 1961 Stranahan finished his Ph.D., moved to Aspen, and completed what he calls "a triumph of creative hucksterism."

Physics in the early '60s reveled in post-Sputnik hysteria. The Cold War dragged on and the public (assisted by politicians) was alarmed that the Russians were first into orbit. Surely the folks who got us the Bomb could get us into space. Of course, the fringes of physics then developing might not have practical application for another hundred years, but its practitioners didn't press the point. The National Science Foundation was joyously handing out grants, complete with overhead and summer salaries, apparently suitable for use in Aspen.

Yet all was not so smooth. Aspen was already embarked on its reputation for evil, and the National Science Foundation, fearing the glare of Congressional heavyweights like Senator William Fulbright upon grant money donated for housing in Gomorrah West, got cold feet. Meanwhile the Aspen Institute insisted on architectural control and instead of open and modest digs, the physicists wound up with Zeiss locks on the doors, cost overruns of $30,000 and a roof that leaked. A trustee who had pledged $20,000 mysteriously welched. The Office of Naval Research came to the rescue, but the building was not ready in time for the physicists. The Aspen Physics Center was launched in 1962 at the Aspen Meadows, with offices in motel rooms, seminars in the marble garden, and that sense of pioneering and adventure that blooms in adversity.

24

After Sputnik, the next red herring to hit the world of physics was a simplistic little essay by C.P. Snow called *Science and the Two Cultures,* in which the nonscientific sector was scolded for not knowing the Second Law of Thermodynamics. Surely the Aspen Institute for Humanistic Studies, with scientists in the side yard, was in a unique position to bring the two cultures together. As George Stranahan describes the episode, a half dozen of the physicists least likely to upset businessmen were selected to read the assigned classics and participate in executive seminars, in the notion that a mutual discussion of the Peloponnesian Wars or *Billy Budd* would shed some obscure light on the relationship between business and physics — a relationship that was otherwise perfectly obvious. One executive, himself an arms manufacturer, mystified physicists by proposing that one of their number be chosen to atone in some undisclosed way for the Hiroshima bomb. There was a panel at which the venerable philosopher Mortimer Adler took on three physicists to prove that the whole is equal to more than the sum of its parts, with the physicists agreeing to anything to speed their way to a beer. The physicists and businessmen arrived in Aspen with stereotypes of each other, the physicists seen as arrogant young Eastern Jewish boys who had Never Met a Payroll, and the businessmen considered remarkable only for their ability to make money, and otherwise distinguished by Palm Beach clothes, young wives and reactionary politics. The images survived the seminars, only to be broken down at dinner, with many a physicist carrying a businessman to his motel room, tucking him in and arranging for volleyball or a picnic next day.

Culture notwithstanding, the Aspen Physics Center flourished to the point where the National Science Foundation braved Senator Fulbright and began extending grants. Meanwhile a physicist named R.R. Wilson, having spent summers here, decided that Aspen was the place to design the National Acceleration Lab proposed for Batavia, Illinois, since here were the physicists who would know what they wanted in the way of an accelerator. Needing conference space for 40 people, Wilson built a second building in 1968 for half the cost of the first building, despite six intervening years of inflation, displaying the kind of austerity he would wield on a grand scale in raising Fermilab. A third building to house a library, seminars and more offices was added in 1978.

If the Aspen Center for Physics is a quiet success, it is largely because of what it lacks. There are no classes to teach, deadlines to meet, bureaucrats to obey, compulsory get-togethers, faculty teas, orientation sessions or social hierarchies. There are no telephones in the offices and even mail, boasts Stranahan, is difficult to get. The Center for Physics provides an atmosphere of relaxed isolation where a physicist may let his ideas play out under ideal conditions, without interruption. The Center works on the premise that science is advanced by letting practitioners go their own way; or, in the words of co-founder Cohen, "contented cows give good milk."

But the Center for Physics is no hermitage. Each physicist shares an office with one other physicist, and uses in common the library, secretarial services and Xerox machines. Seminars are scheduled almost daily, and consist of a participant presenting his work on say, the Fermi-Pasta-Ulam Problem or H-Space, while those who show up may debate the matter for the rest of the day. And here one may meet the giants in one's field, like Murray Gell-Mann, who named and identified quarks, or Phil Anderson in condensed matter physics, and ask without fear their thoughts on lepton scattering, or the problem of pulsar glitches.

Aspen in this regard serves a vital function. Because of the complexity of contemporary physics, with its proliferation of strange disciplines, it is necessarily practiced by specialists. Many physicists spend the rest of the year at isolated universities and laboratories, working alone or with a few colleagues on esoteric problems, and even if they are avid readers of scientific journals it is impossible to keep up. In Aspen physicists collide, and often a specialist who arrives expecting to further his pet project will find his brightest ideas spark off other physicists, so that he is creatively deflected from course, or winds up collaborating. Roger Penrose, one of the pioneers of black hole theory, wrote that his 1976 visit to Aspen "has given me the opportunity to talk to first-class physicists who work in areas different from my own and to discover common interests and methods of approach which I had not been aware of before. There has, hitherto, been rather little opportunity to have detailed discussions with workers in other fields and to exploit the numerous areas of overlap...." Centers like Aspen can expose blind alleys and eliminate a tremendous duplication of effort — a lesson especially painful to one physicist who learned, to his horror, that someone in Finland had already solved the problem to which he had devoted several fruitless years.

It is true that physics, at its top level, is a floating community, with physicists gravitating toward the action, and there are summer programs elsewhere, not to mention the great laboratories with intensive year-around programs. But at Brookhaven, Stanford and Fermilab, the great American centers, one is forced to live on site as the guest of a permanent staff, while CERN (the European Organization for Nuclear Research near Geneva) is so large and impersonal that it dissolves into national cliques. Even the summer programs at such exotic spots as Grenoble, Corsica, Sicily and Brandeis are, in reality, graduate schools with faculty, student body, schedules and a pecking order. In Aspen, on the other hand, Nobel laureates and grad students are treated as equals in terms of office space, housing, secretarial services and the Center's modest facilities. Even the corporation's 24 trustees are mostly working physicists, with a stake in how the Center is run, while a voluntary rotating committee passes on applications. The final melting pot is a fiercely competitive volleyball court, supplemented by brown bag picnics, concerts, the assorted seductions of Aspen, and weekends that find half the participants in the hills where they experience, says Stranahan, a complementary sense of frontier.

Aspen Chain Reaction

Such idyllic conditions have their cost — a popularity which has left the Aspen Center for Physics slightly less democratic than it was. In the early years the Center could accept any qualified applicant, but even with 70 scientists here at a time and more than 200 spread over a summer, in 1979 there were nearly twice as many applications as available spaces. Preference is given to those who have not been here before (and who comprise nearly half the yearly attendance), but their needs must be balanced with regulars who bought homes here, who would lose their grants if they were not extended office space, and every year there seems more to juggle. Nor is physics self-supporting. Major funding comes from the National Science Foundation, with additional help from the National Academy of Sciences, NASA, Bell Laboratories, IBM, Xerox, the Arco Foundation and numerous others. This money supports, among other necessities, three secretaries, three maintenance men, two groundskeepers and an administrator. There is finally the ongoing nightmare of Aspen housing. Two-thirds of the physicists arrive with familes and 80 family rentals must be contracted for three months, a matter handled so adroitly by administrator Sally Mencimer that it cost less in 1979 than 1978 — a talent which Stranahan ascribes to Mencimer's Scottish heritage.

Physics, of course, is a loose term for a spectrum of disciplines, but its progress in this century finds it working with ever smaller units. Particle physics, currently the wildest frontier, was essentially born out of nuclear physics after World War II, consolidated itself during the '60s and is now exploding with infinitesimal knowledge about the basic constituents of the universe. Concerned as it is with the division of atoms into the various quarks and electrons, now believed to be the smallest units of which existence is composed, particle physics is allied with astrophysics, discoverer of pulsars, quasars, radio galaxies and black holes, which test those units under vast and extreme conditions. Attendance at the Center reflects those trends with approximately 40% of the participants in particle physics, 25% in the more traditional condensed matter physics, and the balance scattered in astrophysics, biophysics, plasma physics and other disciplines. Groups, interdisciplinary and otherwise, are organized for the study of particular problems, with invitations extended by the organizer. Occasionally an experimental physicist shows up to confer with the theorists who create the problems. But Aspen reflects the split in physics between theorists and experimentalists, and the physicists here are engaged in formulating the hypotheses which will be tested, accepted or scrapped elsewhere. And it is comforting for locals to know that Aspen physicists, equipped only with desks, are splitting the atom in the safest way possible: conceptually.

Still it must be asked, given funding from federal, corporate and military sources, and given a knowledge of recent history, whether the studies at the Aspen Center for Physics have practical application, and, if so, whether they are all benign. It seems that in condensed matter physics, certain participants, working in the area of thermodynamics to increase the efficiency of machines, hope to have a positive impact on the energy crisis. In other areas, however, physicists seem to be working out of a disinterested passion to find out how the universe works, seem removed from practical considerations, and claim that in some fields any cultural impact might be a century away. Outfits like Arco, Xerox and NASA are willing to fund flights of theory, it seems, partly to have access to the brightest minds on the frontier of physical knowledge, and partly to be in on whatever *might* turn up. Lasers, Telstar and (for good or for ill) nuclear fission have, after all, turned up in the past. The Office of Naval Research, the Center's first funder, is rewarded with reports on what their physicists accomplish and hope to work on next, giving them a useful window on the future. It is also significant that in 1979 Aspen was involved in a unique exchange of eight particle physicists and eight laser and plasma physicists with the Soviet Union, an exchange from which Paul Fishbane, outgoing president of the Aspen Center for Physics, claims to have received useful personal benefit. Because of government sponsorship, it is ironically easier for a Russian than a European physicist to reach Aspen, and further curious, given Aspen's reputation in this country for sex, cocaine and expensive sandwiches, that this is the one spot that looks safe from the Kremlin.

If the disciplines of contemporary physics are so abstruse as to verge on the comic, and practical applications are decades off, of what interest is all this to the general public? The fact is that physics is the science that underlies all the others, and currently seems on the brink of a major new synthesis, the first since the age of Newton. To simplify radically, it is now generally held that the universe is run by four forces: the color force, which holds together the atomic nucleus; the electric force, carrier of light, sustainer of life and the binder between atoms; the weak force, which creates the heavier elements during the death of stars; and gravity. It is also held that the basic particles of the universe are all species of quarks, which compose the atomic nucleus, and the various electrons. What physicists are attempting at this moment, with a mind-numbing elaboration of ideas, is to find how the forces are related to each other, to organize the particles into a coherent and symmetrical system, then to evolve an equation or set of equations that will account for all observable phenomena, large or small, natural or fabricated — equations which would, in sum, explain how everything works.

Considering the extravagance of knowledge now compared with the time of Newton, the endeavor seems mad. Why not tilt at something more solid, like a windmill? But the nuclear, electric and weak forces have already been partially unified, and particles which have been merely conjured to round out the system have — with numberless false starts and scrapped theories — been found to exist. Gravity so far has resisted alliance with the other forces, and Einstein, in fact, spent the latter part of his life working on the problem in vain, partly because his efforts were premature, and partly because he could not accept the Uncertainty Principle ("God," he complained, "does not play dice with the universe."). But some of humanity's brightest minds, extended by computers, sensors for probing the heart of the atom and the margins of space, and laboratories costing billions of dollars, are passionately at work on unification, diligently fitting piece to piece. The elusive equations may come in a few years or elude our species forever, but despite personal ambition and national politics, the effort is a massive and global cooperation to understand. Knowing the religious feelings of Einstein, as well as the lack of them among other prominent physicists, I asked one physicist whether he felt there was any religious content to physics as it is now practiced. He thought a moment, then echoed the thought of Steven Weinberg quoted earlier. "It is the faith that nature is ultimately simple."

Of course, that simplicity, if it *is* found, will only tell us how, not why, and will not answer Heidegger's question of why there is something instead of nothing. It will only establish some ground rules, the stage on which the universe plays itself out. But further implications begin to emerge. It is now fairly certain that our universe began around 15 billion years ago in a primal explosion, a Big Bang, from which all subsequent events flower and disperse. At the instant of the Big Bang the four forces may all have been equal in strength, in a symmetry buried in time; then they burst into their separate functions as the universe flew apart. This division of equal forces may indicate that nature violates its perfection in a precise way — in what Nigel Calder (in *The Key to the Universe*, a book I cannot recommend too highly to those still reading) calls "broken symmetry." With absolute symmetry, the universe would be homogeneous and boring; with no symmetry at all, the universe would be chaotic, incomprehensible and boring. But just as the precise angle of a prism breaks white light into the spectrum of visible color, so does a strategic imbalance break the primal ingredients into a universe so rich it can create an Aspen not only replete with physicists, but also with fundamentalists making the rounds with their creaking predictions, their nostalgic hierarchy of the saved and the damned, their scary little melodrama which doesn't misapprehend the universe so much as it insults it — to pick an example not quite at random.

It is too early to tell whether we may safely storm the gates of ignorance, or whether, as Robinson Jeffers wrote, our little knowledge may have proved too much. Before pure science gives us the answers, applied science may do us in. But if we gain the privilege of looking back on this century, it may be seen as a time when basic information was put together. And if Aspen gets a mention, it may be partly because a low-profile operation helped us become, as a species, not just locals, but citizens at large.

5.

Recycling the Recycler

Charged with feeding the family spaniel, I was required at a tender age to open the can at both ends, push a gooey, evil-smelling pink round of Gaines into the dog dish, peel the lids off both ends, slip them into the hollow cylinder, stamp the can flat, tear off the label and toss the tin into a box for some mysterious disappearance known as the War Effort. That first contact with recycling was an act of faith, without ideology. It was less reassuring 25 years later, after two subsequent wars which spared the family kitchen, to be seated with a group of young locals in the Wheeler Opera House pondering the minerals and fibers being torn in peacetime from forest and field and mountain, processed through factory, market, home and car, then spewed back on fields and oceans and forests of this same earth in the form of trash — frequently missing the dump. It was clear the process could not continue on a finite sphere, could only end in convulsions or be channeled toward regeneration by sober, chastened human beings. But how to begin in a fun-loving dead-end valley?

Earth Day 1971, a year after the event was proclaimed by Wisconsin's Senator Gaylord Nelson, provided the catalyst. While Aspen High School presented educational programs elsewhere, our improvised recycling committee set up a table by the south goalpost of Wagner Park with literature, ready sermons on excessive packaging and closed circuits, and a couple of bins to accept beer bottles and aluminum cans for the ongoing Coors program. The rain fell viciously. We took turns supervising the table. Perhaps five customers blundered by. "If the earth wants to get saved," snarled one volunteer, "the least it could do is cooperate."

But standing in the rain apparently displayed enough zeal that the county offered us a sprawling tin shed right downtown, across from the courthouse and behind the First National Bank. Possessed of real estate, fantasy took flesh. Bins were installed to receive aluminum and Coors bottles to truck to the Coors warehouse in Glenwood Springs, and Rio Grande Motor Way was persuaded to allow their trucks returning empty to Denver to haul newspapers to

Friedman & Sons, the only paper recycling program in several states. More exotic, the county sanitarian agreed to a pit at the county dump to receive glass for experimental glasphalt: a species of asphalt using crushed bottles instead of sand as a base, which would simultaneously dispose of the empties, reduce the need for the sort of operation goring the north bank of the Roaring Fork near Gerbaz, and provide a roadbed tougher and less apt to pothole than the substance we know so well. Never attempted at this elevation, our glasphalt program would actually contribute to Knowledge, and even the sanitarian was excited.

The recycling center was masterminded by Nat Fleck, whose expertise in discriminating shopping and novel uses for over-packaging had reduced his weekly garbage to a matter of ounces. In charge of field work was Dave Hyatt, a bartender with six and a half feet of disquieting brawn, who made the rounds of Aspen's bistros and secured commitments from all but two to comply with the Coors program for commercial establishments. He also carpentered a half dozen bins for strategic placement around town. Kneely Taylor presented City Council with schemes to expand recycling through civil law, while keeping a hand in the sorting duties. Abetted by an enthusiastic committee — one member with an organic soap concession, another who wrote publicity blurbs of attempted wit and occasional rhyme — recycling in Aspen experienced its first flourishing. Then with little warning Nat Fleck took off to become a river guide on the San Juan, Dave Hyatt joined VISTA and was shipped to Boston, Kneely Taylor went to law school in Denver, and the media man was left holding the many, many bags.

Not that I was alone. The recycling committee had been absorbed by the newly formed Environmental Task Force, becoming one of its tentacles, and I had a list of forty names. I encouraged all members to show up at the recycling center when they were in town, to separate aluminum from tin, to straighten and tie newspapers, to smash bottles, sort bags. When results were marginal I assigned people specific days to be responsible for. Chaos matured on schedule. I called meetings. At one meeting a dozen people showed up. At the next there were only two, both of whom had missed the previous meeting so as to insure total discontinuity, and one regaled us over an hour with ethnic jokes. I am not, I have conceded, born to lead.

Meanwhile, the recycling center exerted its fascination. The printed matter was a constant source of wonder and could lure one into hours of compulsive browsing. Besides the Denver dailies and high-circulation magazines, there appeared architectural journals, fan magazines, art reviews, boxes of Xeroxed Montaigne (all the same half-essay), comics, Robert Bly's poetry and a copy of the *New Hungarian Quarterly* I still treasure. Someone dutifully recycled each issue of *Lifeline*, a reactionary publication which revealed the environmental movement to be a Communist plot masterminded by Ralph Nader. One man, bringing in his own selection, inquired about the general span of literary taste as reflected in the recycling center.

"We get everything from German pornography to *The Congressional Record,*" I reported brightly.

"Doesn't sound like much of a range to me," he snorted.

A wide range of lifestyles became apparent — the Purina Chow bags full of bourbon bottles, the TV tray and Dr. Pepper mixes. Also received were items somewhat beyond the program. The City Market bin disgorged a fine sheepskin coat (alas, too large) and a beach towel still serviceable. The center sprouted tangles of coat hangers, automobile parts, rags, Cub Scout uniforms, visquine and, sadly and frequently, pure garbage. The county once dumped several hundred pounds of expired license plates, for which an outlet was ultimately found. I had a fair row with a tourist I caught peeing. And one sweet soul left a full six-pack of Harp Ale. Cynical from too much time at the center, I held it to the light, inspected the labels, felt the caps, sniffed, then took it home. It was delicious.

While most of the trash simply materialized, a few customers outside the committee became visible regulars. A girl had me set aside all the Michelob bottles because they had "such a pretty shape," and several people reported punctually for wine bottles to be cut into drinking glasses, a craze then at its zenith. Some one brought back the used tops strung into a set of interlocking windbells, and left them hanging by the entrance like a miniature pagoda. One young man determined the need for a rack for bundling newspapers, and produced a welded sculpture five feet high, a rectangular stem bursting into a radiant four-petaled flower. It was too small to hold newspapers but would have been distinguished in someone's garden, and the sculptor claimed the recycling center had offered him much-needed therapy. A boy just out of Aspen High School showed up frequently to ask how he could help, and to seek advice on how much of his glistening red hair he would have to chop off to secure a job. Once he showed up mowed to the nub. Mulling the exactitude of his new employer, I explained I had already straightened out but we did need people to pass out Merson literature at the Post Office, if he didn't mind a change.

"I can't," he smiled apologetically." "I've become a Jehovah's Witness and we're not allowed to do anything political."

But the novelty wore off, problems accelerated and the separation of trash lost its glamor. It was relaxing to part aluminum from tin after a hard wrestle with words, and the problem of getting rid of the wrong items, of misunderstood programs when even Coors changed its format a couple of times a year, was not to be begrudged when so many enthusiastic customers had made recycling a way of life. What was less encouraging was to clean up broken glass after local children had thrown the bottles against the wall for sport. Catching them in the act, as occasionally happened, entailed the further complication of informing their parents, of getting caught in family disputes, of supervising while the kids cleaned up at the parents' insistence, shirking to the end.

The Coors recycling program, the melting down of old containers to make new, is a kind of halfway measure not to be confused with a genuine solution, but it was a comparative joy to operate. I borrowed a truck every second or third Saturday for a run to the warehouse in Glenwood Springs, took a certain amount of razzing for the high quotient of Heineken, Tuborg and Carta Blanca bottles which further confirmed the wealthy effeteness of Aspen, then collected the largest checks they paid out, often in excess of $40, payable to the Environmental Task Force.

A harmless interlude was the egg carton caper. A food co-op in Crested Butte let it be known that they needed used egg cartons, and we put out the word. For months the center was strewn with styrofoam harmonicas floating palely among the papers, bottles and cans, a strange algae bloom. At last the co-op showed up, took perhaps three dozen, then vanished forever. Unable to interest the Monastery in recycling them, or musicians in nailing them up for cheap soundproofing, a friend and I hauled them to the dump, where they made an inspiringly soft pile. Seized with sudden folly we took turns swan-diving in their midst. It was their one useful moment.

The glasphalt program suffered a setback when the sanitarian became embroiled in a minor phone and travel expense scandal and found employment downvalley. But the despair, the agony, the invitation to suicide was the attempt to recycle paper. Half of all solid waste is newsprint. It is heavy, shapeless, bulky, slides out of your hands, leaves an oily black smear on all it touches, and only can be handled properly tied, which no one wants to do. All the bad news isn't on the paper; some of it *is* the paper. Rio Grande Motor Way consented to haul our accumulation only when we could fill their largest semi. It took two months to assemble sufficient paper, magazines and cardboard. On the appointed day a driver would back the semi to the recycling center, the cab at the far end of the impound lot across what is now the municipal stable, the back door yawning in anticipation. A work crew, nominally committed in advance and loudly encouraged on the radio, would or would not show up. It would rain if possible. Or snow. Of most dedication was Tom Crum's class from the Community School, but their time was limited. In desperation three or four of us would wind up staggering under armloads of paper for hours, shoulders and backs protesting, to inherit a newsprint cough that dug in like the flu. Rio Grande would report back that their truck had to wait three days to be unloaded at the overstocked plant; meanwhile our net profit — which went to the Boy Scouts, the Visiting Nurses or the Pitkin County Library since Rio Grande refused to recognize our non-profit status — at $7 a ton, was less than $100. To placate Rio Grande I would write an effusive letter of gratitude to the *Aspen Times* after each shipment, which the *Times,* obviously bored, would label under headings like "Thanks Now Official."

All that wouldn't have been so bad, knowing the paper might have spared a few trees, if the two months of accumulation for each load had progressed smoothly. But the joys of newsprint *en masse* were discovered by local gradeschoolers. Younger than the bottle smashers, they contrived elaborate forts of tied bundles, complete

with simulated moats, walls, turrets, secret passageways, in the process breaking the cord or deliberately liberating the units. They held newspaper wars. They would ravish the magazines for *Playboys,* occasionally swiping an issue but usually ripping out the centerfold. They would rifle the bottles for returnables (worth remembering for anyone who thinks deposit legislation doesn't work). I would be crawling over the newspapers to get to the far end and suddenly the labyrinth would collapse. . . .

Awake in the night, my fears grew antlers. Children were playing in the newspapers, their house of cards collapsed, and one would be crushed, or smothered. They were experimenting with matches, smoking one thing or another, and one of Aspen's little ones would go up in flames. They were smashing bottles and glass would dispatch an eye. Away from town, having left the center in someone's nominal care, I would wonder what I would face when I got back: ashes, child blindness, a lawsuit. . . .

One day I got a call from a Girl Scout who explained somewhat shyly that she and a friend were trying to raise funds for a trip to Hawaii: could they install a bin at the recycling center? I explained that all existing programs were covered by the current bins, but perhaps they could find another location in town. Ten minutes after I hung up a bomb went off in my head. I called the girl back: how would you like the WHOLE RECYCLING CENTER? The girl was briefly speechless. Well . . . she would have to consult with her adult supervisor, Fay Ward.

The name hovered, then clicked. My mother had just read an article in *Ladies Home Journal* about this fantastic lady in Aspen who operated out of a wheelchair: did I know her? Fay, to my delight and relief, took command after one minor hesitation. "What if it turns out I can't handle it?"

"Pass it on to the Boy Scouts," I suggested, perhaps overeagerly.

Fay managed the program for over three years, netting a dependable $30 a month from the Coors program, with annual bonanzas from the Deaf Camp Picnic, and she and the girls, with supplemental funds, finally made it to Hawaii. She too found recycling unpredictable, infuriating and utterly addictive. The bottle smashers maintained their sneak attacks, and the new sanitarian, informed of the glasphalt program upon arrival, later professed ignorance and the scheme died (though the glass pit at the dump may be of interest to future archeologists). Some one left, with motives perhaps best not looked into, a bag of human hair. Spring runoff continued to churn the ground to a small Saragasso of refuse and slush, which now mired

Fay's wheelchair. The County threatened to replace the sheds with something more respectable, and for months Fay pled to be kept informed, to have a spot in urban renewal. Arriving one morning to find the roof had been collapsed onto the bins, she abandoned her wheelchair and crawled under the rubble to retrieve $30 worth of bottles and cans. While recycling customers floundered for a depository, Fay haunted the County another four months for a new location, and was at last gifted with a splendid raised gazebo fronting the alley, for $1,800, which unfortunately she couldn't get into. But the gazebo did provide Fay and me one moment of glory. One morning I received a call from Commissioner Michael Kinsley, asking me to show up at the gazebo that afternoon. "But I'm out of recycling," I complained.

"It will only take a moment," he persisted.

I arrived to find the county commissioners, Fay, reporters and a few bystanders assembled for a small ceremony. After a brief introduction, Kinsley produced a wooden plaque that read, "Fay Ward — Bruce Berger Memorial Recycling Center," and affixed it to the building. But recycling itself didn't thrive in its memorial phase, for the program shrank, then died a couple of years later, and the plaque was removed to discourage unwanted deposits. While it lasted, however, I was able to lead visitors into the alley, show them that I had a building named for me without even having died, and that it was filled, appropriately, with junk.

While our volunteer programs did recycle solid matter, we never suffered delusions we were inflicting anything so grand as a dent in our Fleetwood to oblivion. All recycling in Aspen, of course, falls in the shadow of Freddie Fisher, scavenger saint and jazz alchemist, whose feats with trash will not be equalled by the vulgar. Our real goal was educational, to prepare the kind of citizen who can salvage the future, in the hope we were not recycling things so much as attitudes. If our efforts in any way fostered a climate in which the City and County could undertake a comprehensive program with public support, then the hours of mucking around, the backaches, the insomnia, the visions of children flaming and blinded, even the mountain of egg cartons and the pit of crushed glass will have been worth it. And recyclers themselves are only too glad to suffer the process and leave it to the pros.

6.

Saturday Morning Fever

The first symptoms coincide with the publication of the *Aspen Times* on Thursday afternoon. While some turn desperately to the Help Wanted and For Rent columns, a few flip nervously to see if they are listed in Marriages Dissolved or the Police Blotter and still others are getting the editorials behind them, a curious cross-section turns to a small column labeled Garage Sales. For them the week is hurtling to a climax.

Sometime on Friday the anxious hand tears out the section and plans the attack. The most crucial sales are scheduled for Saturday morning, clustered around ten o'clock, though a few strays seldom worth attending are listed for Friday or Sunday. Taking into account the time and location so as to minimize wasted motion, one numbers the sales in optimum order of attendance. It is helpful to underline times and addresses and look up unfamiliar streets on the map of Aspen in the back of the phone book, and in ordering sales which begin at the same time one must compromise between location and projected quality. The planning of an itinerary, in fact, involves complicated adjustments of time, space and estimated merit, and primes one's nerves for the impending challenge.

Only novices and the chronically late arrive at a garage sale on time; the experts go early. It is never too soon to crash a sale, to turn it, with charm and *chutzpah,* into a pre-sale. I recently arrived 40 minutes early at a particularly hot listing, noted a dozen people apparently setting up, and read a sign on the gate saying, "Don't Bother Us Until 10." Sympathizing with their dilemma, I invaded some lesser ten o'clock sales, then returned on the dot — to find that all but two of the dozen people were customers who had skimmed off the cream.

The term *garage sale* is a slight misnomer, since fewer than a third actually involve garages, and in fact in the East they are known as yard or lawn sales; and in the Southwest, patio sales. But the breadth of junk is the same. One can find, often in flawless condition, clothes, furniture, china, flatware, antiques, kitchen appliances, bedding, towels, televisions, stereos, books, plants, sinks, even cars — everything one needs to brave the 20th century. There are even bargains on such ephemera as twine, Baggies, bungee cords, Ziploc bags and Band-Aids, and certain customers furnishing new homes are shopping solely for basics.

But the utility hounds usually quit once the house is properly appointed, and do not comprise the hard core. The genuine fever case might pick up something useful if the price is sufficiently ridiculous, but is really out for harmonicas, aviator goggles, anvils, ruby drinking glasses, back issues of *Life* and *Batman*, puka shell necklaces, meat grinders, scimitars, cactus lamps: all that is embraced by the word *treasure*. Vendibles have included coffins, missiles, false teeth, bronzed ponies' hooves, and a complete collection of the Watergate issues of *Newsweek*, and an habitué is never offended by anything he sees. Old-timers enjoy watching former possessions migrate from yard to yard, and garage sales are surely the most joyful mode of recycling yet conceived. And the most satisfying purchase, any addict will tell you, is the item you didn't know you wanted, caught sight of, and would die for. Every so often someone will throw a garage sale without having attended one, and will ask you on arrival what you're looking for. The only response is to look your accuser in the eye and reply, "a good time."

Garage sales have no ethics except to honor the Eighth Commandment, Thou shalt not steal, but it is considered bad form to take them too seriously. A former Aspenite demonstrated bad form to the extent that she would grab, with shaking hand, anything another customer cast an eye upon, as if she were cast as Greed in a morality play. My friend Abigail recalls arriving early at a sale and asking the vendor if she had any jewelry. The lady went upstairs and returned with a small box. Greed materialized over Abigail's shoulder. Abigail could see that it was costume jewelry, not especially valuable, and asked, "How much for the box?"

"Fifteen dollars."

"I'll take it," said Abigail.

"I'll give you twenty-five!" interjected Greed.

"You can't do that," burst Abigail, then on reconsideration selected the six best pieces and said to the lady, "How about eight dollars for these?"

"Sure," the lady replied, and accepted the cash.

Greed, seeing she was left with the dregs, said, "But you can have the whole *box* for fifteen." Abigail took her six jewels and left.

But ugly moments are rare and Saturday morning is in fact a floating party. The same faces turn up every week and one gets to know them — the waitress with a passion for old bottles, the kid with the turban, the writer with the skull collection. Every element of so-called society is represented, and if there is a common trait, it is a polite eccentricity. A few years back a pair of on-duty police would check out the sales with the motor running: if one is never surprised by the merchandise, one is never startled by the customers. A conniving subculture evolves. Strangers hovering in search of an address, or converging at a sale which has been canceled, recognize each others' bewilderment, roll down the windows and tie up traffic while they debate the next move. Because Aspen is still small and those who plan itineraries come up with similar routes, Aspen garage sales have generated what Kurt Vonnegut in *Cat's Cradle* calls a *karass* — a group of people related by real psychic brotherhood rather than the fact, say, that they were all born in Indiana.

In addition to its social features, on an average Saturday the house tour includes old cabins, condominiums, Jacuzzi chateaux and hideouts never before seen, and I always drag house guests along for an intimate look at the Aspen behind the mask. I find, after 28 years, that I am even learning the names of the streets. I can spout such arcana as that West End Avenue is at the extreme east end of town, and, by dint of missing a sale, that Riverside Avenue is distinct from Riverside Drive. I have learned to distinguish between such gibberish as Timber Ridge, Park Meadows, Stonebridge, Woodstone and Mountain Valley, and when asked for Durant I can rattle it off like any tourist.

There is, of course, a vast difference between Saturdays, between sales, even between seasons. In winter sales stop because of snow, and in summer they suffer from competition with the other arts. Garage sales are primarily off-season events, blossoming in spring and fall. There are sales one could do without: flashy ads that lure you to five battered sneakers and two TV tables, condominium sales that feature beige towels and conservative drinking tumblers (usually with zebras), and sales promising free wine and which turn out not to exist, leaving the victim to scour the facing windows for the trace of a smirk behind a curtain. At the other extremity is an extravaganza that occurs every two years in Aspen's poshest garage, at which dozens of leather boots and jackets, silk shirts and expensive dresses are suspended in parallel racks, with chic miscellany underneath. Iced champagne greets the guest on the way in, a cash register manned by the owner punches him out, and a security guard can be seen dawdling in the drive. All the leather jackets are the same size (not mine) and the occasion makes me feel creepy, though I usually manage to choke down a little champagne.

Most dangerous are the sales in the middle, which have been my ruin. Several years ago some friends in Phoenix planned a Kitschmas party at which the gifts were to be true kitsch — items in bad taste with a utilitarian value — as opposed to schlock, which is merely decorative. I started my shopping in June, and by the time we were gathered under the yuletide yucca, I had amassed a transistor radio in the form of a schooner, a toilet paper rack which played *Auf Wiedersehen* on a music box when pulled, a cat-shaped clock with rolling eyeballs and a pendulum tail, a lamp in a miniature cable car, a vintage Coors wastebasket, and a rhinestone-encrusted can opener from Las Vegas, enabling me to hold my own. My most breathtaking moment, however, occurred in response to a sale that had begun hours before. I bicycled from sign to sign, spotted a single item on a card table, and gasped. Could it actually be the rare Stereo-Realist camera I'd been chasing for years, obsolete, worth hundreds of dollars? It was, in mint condition. I paid the man five dollars and fled.

But pride of possession is often a mistake. Once someone offered the seller ten dollars for my fine bicycle. Another time I paid

five dollars for a lime green porcelain bowl. "I'm so glad it's found a new owner," gushed the lady. "It's always been one of my favorites."

"I'm delighted too," I said. "I've been looking for a new dog dish."

She congealed. "You're going to let a *dog* eat out of that?" Protestations that the bowl's new service would guarantee it permanent display proved ineffective.

Triumph is sweet but a day of bad sales leaves a hollow, and those who missed their quota may dash to the Aspen Thrift Shop or a consignment emporium like Cheap Shots. And success itself takes unlikely forms. A friend who feels she has Bought Enough considers it a successful day when she has resisted everything — though she wouldn't stay home for fear of missing something. And all garage salers relish post-mortems, bragging about their conquests, lamenting the ones that got away, and one junkist reserves Saturday afternoon for playing with her new toys, for repairing, installing, washing, or just turning them over in her hands. She particularly likes to buy tarnished silver and polish it, which gives her a sense of bringing flowers out of the mud.

Related phenomena, sacred to all scavengers, are the two church sales. The lesser of the two, the Episcopal Church Bargain Box sale, accepts articles on consignment as well as donations and is overwhelmed by women's clothes, which crowd all else to the margins. So much is the Bargain Box a women's event that women, presumably buying for absent males, elbow the men from their own meager rack of shirts. In revenge I would gladly hold women off from a rack of dresses if I did not fear for my reputation, and possibly my health. While sales are democratic as regards the individual, they are also bastions of sexism.

The transcendent event is the biannual Community Church sale, whose opening charge is Aspen's answer to the running of the bulls at Pamplona. Begun by church-going garage salers Elmer and Esther Beamer, they are intended less as fund-raisers than as a community service, a way to discard things so that the needier can acquire them cheaply. Elmer, who mans one of the cash boxes, confesses to feeling invigorated when people delight in what they buy.

All year donations are stashed in the top hall and the little-used church balcony, behind and under the pews, and two months before each sale the minister removes his car from the parsonage garage to make way for stored furniture. More than 60 volunteers, member and nonmember alike, prepare for the great day, and those who log more than eight hours get to buy ahead of time. An evangelical fringe benefit, reports Beamer, is that some nonmembers become interested in the church and wind up joining. Items are priced at a quarter of their estimated *garage sale* value — which is to say they are practically given away — and donations too lavish for the sale are sold in separate ads.

The Beamers, moving to Aspen from a wealthy bedroom community, were appalled at some of the donations, and further appalled when they actually sold. They realize that some people donate because the church is closer than the city dump, but have learned there is nothing too humble for a price tag.

Nearing countdown it is impossible to park within blocks, and approaching on foot one hears a commotion like Caesar's rabble. The mood resembles a nightclub about to explode, and in the early years, when workers were allowed to pre-select up to the wire, one girl was heard to say, "Mama, those bastards are taking all the best toys!" When the church bell tolls on the stroke of ten and the barricades are unrolled, a mob pours through like lava and disperses toward children's items on the left, books, records and men's clothing on the right, women's clothing downstairs, and a sublime agglomeration in the sanctuary. The next hours are pandemonium. One friend has given up casing the sanctuary for fear of being trapped in the pews. Money takers are given no nickels or pennies and are instructed to bargain upward when correct change is impossible, rounding off to the next dollar if the customer is looking flush. Among my own miracles are a small stuffed iguana for a dime, a plastic palm tree, and an ancient ten-inch LP of some Aaron Copland piano music I was wrestling with, performed by the composer. After an hour one feels like a bandit seeking asylum in the streets.

Nor is the escapade finished when the sale officially ends at one thirty. The Aspen Police accompany Elmer Beamer to the bank with the take — $7,200 and $6,900 from the 1979 spring and fall sales respectively, money which goes toward church operating expenses or special projects like a new roof. What remains unsold is picked up by the Methodist Church of Basalt, and what they can't sell goes to the Salvation Army in Grand Junction, which can sell anything. As the first sale was being dismantled and the Beamers were standing by a bedspring which was leaning against a tree, a young man showed up, chagrined to have missed the sale. "You can still buy this bedspring," said Elmer.

"Can I really? How much?"

"Thirty-five cents."

"But I'm serious. I really want to buy it," insisted the young man.

"He's telling you that it's thirty-five cents," said Esther.

"I'll tell you what, I'll give you a dollar," said the young man in exasperation, and hauled away the bedspring in a state of bliss. A less friendly post-mortem occurred when the parsonage was broken into and searched the night after the sale, apparently under the delusion that the proceeds were stuffed in the parson's mattress.

It's hard to imagine recreation so unblemished as the pursuit of junk. I've heard tell of a lady in Denver whose seven-room house is filled to the ceiling with garage sale acquisitions, to the degree that one has to walk sideways from room to room and only one burner of her four-burner stove is open for business — and still she makes the rounds. One wonders whether her insurance agent knows, and as with the case of Greed, one suspects serious problems. A recent *Denver Post* editorial inveighed against the signs left up afterward, and it is true that along with recycling the sales generate a bit of thoughtless litter. But as for the expense, between spectacular savings and the fact that what you buy by mistake you can unload for as much at a sale of your own, the pastime is almost lucrative. And as for the more serious charge of materialism, the truth is that garage sales, by lumping microwave ovens and Dior dresses with lunch boxes and beer mugs in one curbside stew, have a curious way of deflating the vainer selections. The ruthless leveling of all merchandise is, in reality, anti-materialist. What motivates the hardened garage saler at heart is not avarice but incurable lust for the variety of this world.

But is the garage sale, as earlier suggested, truly an art form? Critic Susan Sontag has written, "Recall that it was Breton and other surrealists who invented the second hand store as a temple of vanguard taste and upgraded visits to the flea market into a mode of aesthetic experience." And American poet Wallace Stevens sees in "The Man on the Dump" a poetic prototype, a sort of junk collector who finds "the dump/ Is full of images," and from this world's refuse writes

> *. . . the janitor's poems*
> *Of every day, the wrapper on the can of pears,*
> *The cat in the paper bag, the corset, the box*
> *From Esthonia: the tiger chest, for tea . . .*
> *One feels the purifying change. One rejects*
> *The trash . . .*

At the hub of a global recreational crossroads, magpies of the 20th century, Aspenites have access to scraps of most of the world's surviving cultures, its instantaneous history, its exotic refuse. The town is small enough to encompass in a single morning, and full of people with exotic tastes living beyond their means, poised to turn their follies into instant cash. The Aspen garage saler is a person on a most privileged dump. The art of the twentieth century, with its blitz of merchandise, media and personal choice, is, after all, the art of collage. From here, from there, out of this and that, with relish, humor and taste, one assembles a life. That box from Esthonia, perhaps. One rejects the trash. . . .

7.

Wings and Wild Hungers

My favorite local bird, after the red-tailed hawk, is the magpie.
Why I should identify more with raptors and scavengers than, say,
songbirds is better explored on the couch than on the page, but some
quality of feistiness, of unholy leaping and shrieking, of assumption
that the world was made for the sole abuse of magpies, strikes a
wistful chord in my marrow. Perhaps magpies are the innocent brats
we would still like to be.

Even detractors admit they are handsome. Averaging twenty
inches long, slender, elegant as dragonflies, magpies are a study in
black and white until the sun flashes their black with teal blue and
emerald — a fact not lost on Audubon, whose down-swooping
magpie unfolds like an arc of color wheel. And magpies have a
literary career as venerable as the nightingale, beginning with the
Greek legend of the nine daughters of Pireus, King of Emathia, who
challenged the nine muses to a singing contest: they lost and for their
presumption were turned into magpies. Chaucer's lecherous and
tyrannical Wife of Bath was said to be "jolly as a pie," and James Joyce
mocked the phoenix legend in *Finnegans Wake* by calling it a
"magpyre." Magpies have been kept as pets, and if their tongues are
split they can be taught to speak like parrots. Called *urraca* in
Spanish — a name more resonant of their character — they range
from Pitkin County through Europe, Asia, and North Africa, devouring insects, seeds, fresh carrion, eggs and the young of lesser birds.
They benefit agriculture by preying on grasshoppers and rodents
which in turn prey on crops, and they benefit motorists by removing
road kills. They prefer their meat well-aged. Like the cockroach, the
pigeon and the starling, the magpie is one of the universals.

Until lately my yard was graced with a magpie nest which
completely encircled the tops of three clustered Norwegian spruce
trees. Comprised of loose twigs bound by a mud floor, scenic and
shoddy in the manner of Aspen housing, the nest turned out a new
brood every year. It was the highlight of my spring to watch the
fledglings, nearly as large as their parents, leave their nest squawking

like cheap New Year's favors, swooping from one aspen branch to another while mama ran a savage interference.

But magpies in general, and mine in particular, are not popular on my corner. I even have a small grudge of my own, involving an assortment of sand dollars, pelican shells and sea urchins that was arrayed along my inner sill — until the afternoon I returned from errands through my chronically open door, to find a magpie in full attack. My German shepherd, long used to running magpies from his own bone collection, dozed nearby with the hospitality of the senile. Nothing on the sill was edible even to a scavenger, but the smell of old sea meat must have been maddening. And while the bird leapt squawking and shrieking, vast among the stricken shells, its companion followed every prance along the outside sill, mimicking gestures exactly, stabbing the glass that walled out the feast. When I reached for an empty wastebasket the magpie swooped to my lamp and shat grandly. After several passes I cornered the bird between the basket and the window, slid a large thin book over the top, and jockeyed the bundle to the door, where the magpie shot skyward in a blast of loose feathers. The image of that dance on the sill, the envy without mocking the greed within, is what survives of my shells.

I can forgive the magpies their lapses, but my friends across the way will never absolve them from doing in the vireos that nested in their chimney. As killers of songbirds I would personally rate them well below plate glass windows and stray cats from the Villas, but I am indulgent of my own. In any case magpies and vireos are prey to the same god, and who am I to judge?

But my scavengers have a more formidable opponent, a horsey

neighbor we will refer to as Local Velvet. It isn't only that magpies go for her poodle's bones, and when Gigi runs them off they sneak up from behind and stab her in the little pink rosette. It isn't just that they demolish most of the suet Miss Velvet puts out for the orioles and tanagers, and occasionally kill and eat the heart out of a chick before her eyes. It is their unpardonable folly to light on her horses, peck at their sores and consume their equine flesh.

Supportive testimony is mixed. Trudi Peet, boarding horses professionally between Basalt and Carbondale, is unaware that magpies attack open sores, and feels the bird may actually help the horses by devouring harmful insects. Zebulon Pike, writing in 1806 and quoted by Bailey and Neidrach in *Birds of Colorado*, complained that his pack horses "were attacked by magpies, which attracted by the scent from their sore backs, alighted on them and in defiance of their wincing and kicking, picked many places quite raw." The Forest Service must have sided with Pike, for years ago there was a bounty on magpies of a nickel a bird, and the ranger used to lend out a wire cage measuring four by six feet, which lured the birds through a one-way funnel toward suet inside, allowing the trapper to enter through a separate door and club them to death. The bounty has long since been lifted, and the Forest Service disclaims current knowledge of any trapping device. As a migratory bird the magpie is now on the Department of Wildlife protected list, but a loophole as large as the law allows magpies to be killed without a permit if they are "committing or about to commit depredations upon ornamental or shade trees, agricultural crops, livestock or wildlife, or when concentrated in such numbers as to constitute a health hazard or other nuisance." I would hesitate to be a magpie's defense lawyer.

But magpies do have their friends — among them biologist Bob Lewis, who has trained them to come for food at the sound of his whistle and has turned them into beggars. They are one of the truly communal birds, he says, to the extent that the flock sleeps in a single heap, a continuous feather comforter that keeps their body temperature at 104 degrees. He believes that a pecking order determines the sequence in which they prey, and is devising a means of dyeing them to confirm the theory. Once he watched a flock of starlings from downvalley move into his magpies' territory. The leader singled out an intruder and caught the bird in his talons while the rest of the flock shrieked encouragement. The starling slipped away, the magpie dove back at him midair, stabbed him at the base of the skull, and the flock proceeded to devour him. The Wildwood ecosystem has not since been bothered by starlings.

My own brood's territory was as fiercely tended, and Miss Velvet kept me well informed of their activities on her side of the fence. Not my magpies, I protested, God's magpies; mine only on loan. But local tension ran sufficiently high that once after breeding season I actually permitted a person in the employ of Miss Velvet to remove, for a bottle of my scotch, the offending nest. No birds were actually damaged. But whether I felt more keenly the loss of the magpies themselves, or my moral collapse in paying for the removal of creatures I valued for the sake of mere social peace — is a knot I have yet to untangle.

It was, of course, my secret hope that the birds would sneak back and rebuild, but they took their eviction to heart. Several smaller nests still extant high in my cottonwoods have not, to my knowledge, produced in recent years, and my springtimes are boringly silent. It may seem perverse to miss being awakened daily by what sounded like drunken revelry, and to wish on the neighborhood a creature so contemptuous of local values. But to their admirers magpies redeem themselves by brute enthusiasm, by sheer zeal for being brilliant, inventive, arrogant, greedy, flesh-eating magpies. Robinson Jeffers, for whom God and the process of life were synonymous, put the sentiment exactly when he said, in one of his last poems,

Justice and mercy
Are human dreams, they do not concern the birds nor
the fish nor eternal God,
However — look again before you go.
The wings and wild hungers . . .
they are beautiful?
That is their quality: not mercy, not mind, not goodness,
but the beauty of God.

8.

The Littlest Junkies

My piano teacher had cleverly instructed me to practice exercises for "not more than an hour a day," with the perverse result that I did not want to do them for *less* than an hour a day. I was to sit perfectly calm with all ten fingers touching the keys, press one finger of each hand to the bottom of the keyboard, perform symmetrical patterns with the remaining eight, then change the held finger and repeat, but always relaxed, never forced, never loud, letting motion accelerate on its own.

Such practicing required nothing of the eyes, and fortunately there was a new hummingbird feeder just outside the window for them to wander to. Zinging in and out, sipping nectar and defending territory, was a succession of rufous and broad-tailed hummingbirds miraculously hanging in front of the holes, sitting midair at the center of their blurred wings: a vortex of motion too fast for the eye to follow. Practicing in a semi-trance, eyes out the window and fingers on the monotonous keys, senses blurred until I knew what my teacher wanted of me: it was to have hummingbirds for hands.

Years back I had hung up a feeder, but the dish broke and I never bothered to replace it. I waited several days for the first bird to find the new one, advertising it with a huge red plastic carnation left by one of my tackier renters. One morning when I was on the phone to my friend Pierre, arguing lunch spots, I gave an irrelevant shriek. A male rufous, my favorite of all hummers, a cobweb of fire, was my first customer.

Pierre was his cool self. "If you have a male rufous, that's probably the *only* hummingbird you'll get."

But the rufous was merely the greediest of many. It is a little disconcerting that while the host turns contemplative, his guests turn immediately into junkies. Hummingbirds cease to be relaxing when the sugar water runs out. The bird tries every hole in succession, performs a slow spiral up the tube, glares once in the window, then vanishes. Should I drop everything to boil another fix? At one point I moved the feeder to a window at the corner so I could practice without a crook in the neck, wondering whether it would take several more days for the birds to relocate. I watched until a hummingbird arrived at empty space, circled it precisely for half a minute as if it couldn't believe the free lunch had disappeared, spotted the new location and impaled its beak in the nearest hole without bothering to aim. Relocation took seven minutes. Later that day I saw perhaps the same broad-tail scan the eaves on all four sides, as if the house sprouted feeders the way an apple tree sprouts apples.

The voracity of hummingbirds is such that the feeder is the crux of an infernal game of tag as each chases the other from its own sweet territory, their wings ringing like distant telephones, their meals as innocent as the London blitz. Often a bird will scare off another without pausing for nectar, just to prove a point. The rufous, in fact, sits like a bulldog on a nearby twig, sips at leisure, and dive-bombs all comers as if to say, "Get the hell away from *my* flower!" At my neighbors' feeder a vicious bee fends off the birds. Small and non-threatening creatures are cute as long as we admire them in safety, but on their own level they are deadly as the Pentagon. God is not Walt Disney. "The ant's a centaur in his dragon world," said Ezra Pound, imagining insects on their own scale. And the hummingbird's a cruise missile.

Emily Dickinson, writing before hummingbirds had been scientifically studied, thus described a ruby-throated:

> *A route of evanescence*
> *With a revolving wheel;*
> *A resonance of emerald,*
> *A rush of cochineal;*
> *And every blossom in the bush*
> *Adjusts its tumbled head, —*
> *The mail from Tunis, probably,*
> *An easy morning's ride.*

She was smart to hedge with her *probably,* since hummingbirds are native only to the Western Hemisphere, and rightly did not apologize for her cochineal, a red dye derived from the dried female bodies of a Central American insect. And if hummingbirds do not commonly zip from Concord to Tunis, they often make similar jaunts. All hummers living in temperate climates are migratory, wintering in Mexico, Central or South America, and can jet 500 miles on a gram of stored fat.

Hummingbirds are in fact so intricate they seem transistorized. The largest, at 8-1/2 inches, still weighs less than an ounce, yet they beat their wings up to 80 times per second while hovering, and 200 times per second in their courtship dives. Their wings actually swivel in their sockets so that the wingtop faces up on the upbeat, down on the downbeat. The bird gets equal propulsion from each direction and, in a sense, treads air. For its size a hummingbird burns ten times as much energy as a running human being, and must refuel every fifteen or twenty minutes. Even at rest on a perch they are bobbing and alert, always in motion, faintly squeaking like mice. Hyperactive by day, their metabolic rate drops to a tenth the level by night, a torpor they can maintain in cold weather while awaiting a food supply.

The evolution of hummingbirds is not established, but it is believed they began as insect eaters who wound up exploiting the flower. They still consume insects for protein, but are powered by the nectar they draw through two long tubes in their tongues, which you can actually see darting like the tongues of snakes if you stand close to the feeder. Certain flowers, all of them red, have come to depend on them for pollination. Hummingbirds are polygamous and sexist, with the female building the nests, hatching and feeding the young while the male watches, protectively but from a safe distance. After two weeks' incubation, the brood of two is hatched naked and blind, but after three more weeks they are nearly as large as their parents, have no need of flight instruction, and are ready to zoom off forever.

Aspen, with two varieties swarming to hundreds of feeders, seems like hummingbird city. The broad-tail arrives mid-May, breeds locally and stays through the summer, while the rufous, the northernmost of all hummingbirds, breeds as far north as Alaska and merely pauses here a few weeks on its way south. Colorado, with three other migrant hummers, can indeed look down on all America east of Nebraska, where Emily Dickinson's ruby-throated is the sole species. But we are no match for Ecuador, which has 163 of the some 320 species known worldwide. Hummingbirds do have their limitations, being unable to walk or climb let alone play the piano. And a broad-tail which a neighbor brought over after it struck the kitchen window, and whose throat turned dull brown from any angle but straight-on, proved what I'd read — that iridescence rather than pigmentation gives them the greatest concentration of color outside a gem collection.

When I hung up my first feeder, back in the organic '60s, I used honey instead of sugar. If refined sugar causes obesity, diabetes and heart attacks in humans, why extend it to our friends? I have since learned that honey is too strong and will burn out their systems. Sugar water, properly mixed, approximates the nectar of flowers, is immediately metabolized and doesn't linger enough to do them ill. The Arizona Nature Conservancy, whose Ramsey Canyon Preserve nurtures fourteen species and is modestly known as The Hummingbird Capital of America, has issued instructions in their spring 1979 Bulletin. While it is gauche to end a meditation with a recipe, here is their advice:

> *Solution:* Use 3-5 parts water to one part white granulated sugar. Do not use honey. Boil water first, mix, then cool. Do not use food coloring. Change all food, if not taken, every five days.

> *Washing:* Clean feeders at least once a week. Use baby bottle brushes, hot water and no detergent. Vinegar may be used to help remove stubborn mold.

Placement: Try to avoid heavy traffic areas and all-day sun exposure. Placement near a tree for perching is recommended. Experiment with distances apart and numbers of feeders to avoid too many territorial battles.

Miscellaneous Problems: For ants, try petroleum jelly, salad oil, Ben Gay, Vicks Vapor Rub, or other gooey, stinky substances on surfaces leading to the feeder, especially the string or wire hanger. For bees, try a bee guard on the feeder tube tip. Do not add protein supplement to the sugar solution. If the solution freezes, thaw immediately. Keep feeders out of reach of cats.

To which I would only add that the hummingbirds' habit is easier to support than it sounds, and will leave you with withdrawal symptoms of your own when the birds abandon you in September.

9.

Stalking the
Brown-Capped Rosy Finch

We are used to visitors who reach us from remote corners to gape at such local monuments as Maroon Lake, Independence Pass, and John Denver. More cryptically marked are the folks who put themselves to the same effort and expense to make their way through our thinning atmosphere, beyond the last trees, onto the open rocks, to peer through binoculars not at the panorama, but at what appear to be other rocks nearby. If they are lucky, their lenses will bring some drab little creatures into focus. They will make marks in a notebook, and without bothering to finish off the peak they have nearly scaled, they will head back down, their trip to the Rockies a success. Birders (formerly known, more passively, as birdwatchers) will do anything to log a new species.

I had been birding semi-seriously for years before I learned that Colorado had its own endemic bird — a species that can only be seen within our borders, with minor spillovers to Northern New Mexico and Southern Wyoming. The brown-capped rosy finch is supposed to be common once you have struck its habitat, but even so, I didn't encounter it until the third attempt, in a high basin between American Lake and Hayden Peak. Its presence was signaled by faint cries, pairs of hoarse little semi-quavers on a single note. Soon I spotted a sparrowlike bird with a conical, seed-eating bill, poking along the edge of a snowfield. Gradually I realized I was surrounded by finches, as if they had coalesced from the tundra. Heads to the ground, waddling more than hopping, they ignored me with an almost myopic busyness. The female was the classic plain brown bird only a specialist could identify, while the male seemed to show coloration in reverse, with its bright rose hidden in the underparts rather than flaunted on the head and breast. No two males seemed to have the same configuration of rose, and the variations showed best when underlit by the bright snow. Typically, the rose of the underbelly, flecked with dark feathers, lapped onto the shoulders, then

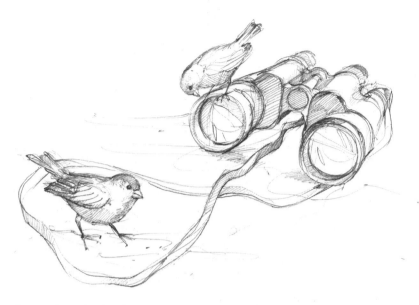

gleamed on the back in a pink line where the wings didn't quite meet. The effect was haphazard, as if the bird had taken a rouge bath. The finches fed obliviously, almost too close for binoculars, until my movement released their vaguely undulant flight.

The brown-capped rosy finch has fine-tuned itself for life in the heights, at least during the warmer months. In early April flocks move from the valleys to their nesting grounds over 12,000 feet and begin to break into pairs. The female selects the site of the nest, a bulky cradle of mosses, grass, feathers, fur, and hair wedged between rocks or set in the niches of cliffs. A clutch of four or five white, pear-shaped eggs appears in early summer. The young are hatched after two weeks of incubation and fed by the parents for another three weeks. When conditions permit, there is a second brood. Diet for adults and young consists of tundra seeds, supplemented by seeds and insects blown onto snowbanks during the year, and progressively revealed as the snow recedes. As soon as all the young are on their own, the flocks begin to regather and move back down, though rarely below 6,000 feet. Like the deer and the elk, their migration is purely altitudinal. Brown-cappeds may roost with up to three other rosy finch species in flocks of up to a thousand birds, cramming themselves into abandoned swallow nests, entrances to caves and mines, railroad tunnels — anywhere they can nestle together and stay out of the wind. Locally they have discovered the eaves of the barn by the turnoff to St. Benedict's Monastery, and in dire weather they even ravage the feeders in town.

If such data on their life cycle seems a little antiseptic, one can turn to the earlier writers, who imagined what it would be like to *be* a bird when the facts ran thin. An unsigned entry on brown-capped rosy finches from a 1940 edition of *Birds of America*, perhaps carried from previous editions, declares the bird to be "optimistic." After disposing of the known particulars, the author continues, "They hunt for the chilled insects and seeds along the edge of the melting snows, and they may be seen with their feathers fluffed, their faces turned toward the wind, busily hopping about and picking up their food, all the time cheerily chattering. Occasionally one will take shelter behind a stone or lump of snow and warm his toes against his warm little body." If such plaintiveness no longer seems quite professional, the projection of human sympathies into a creature of unknowable sensation at least gives us a feel, beyond mere knowledge, for a species' obscure destiny.

Such destinies will naturally provoke yawns from the folks who can only identify peacocks and fried chicken, but even so noted an alpine ecologist as Aspenite Stuart Mace, when asked about the brown-capped rosy finch, replied that he "just never got around to learning little birds." What, then, motivates someone traveling across the continent to glimpse the same feathered nobody?

Many, alas, are expanding what is known as a life-list, a compilation of all the species of birds seen by an individual in a lifetime. As the list swells, so does the rapacity of the birder to add new "lifers" to the pile. Bores of the bird world, the fixated listers lose interest in a bird already identified; like Don Juan, they are only interested in the next one-time thrill. Their real interest is words not birds, and their goal is a swelling of imaginary territory consisting of all the species that have bounced light into their eyes. When they tell you they have seen 1,447 of the world's some 8,600 species of birds, you wonder whether they have actually *seen* any birds at all.

Thus the brown-capped rosy finch, curious in its own right, has become a sitting duck for the quantity buffs who need to check off something new. Dr. Richard Beidleman, probably Colorado's leading ornithologist, tells of a marine biologist who drove from Oregon to collect our bird, and even lined up rangers at Rocky Mountain National Park to lead him into brown-capped rosy finch country. A thunderstorm struck as he arrived, and the biologist, traumatized by a previous encounter with lightning, drove straight back to Oregon without getting out of the car. Dr. Beidleman himself ran into the biologist the following summer in the Flat Tops on his second, and successful, trip to sight the brown-capped rosy finch. Multiply such eccentricity by the abundance of life-listers and you will see that, among other considerations, the brown-capped rosy finch represents a substantial if uncomputed boost to our economy. Local birders are quick to tell you that the brown-capped rosy finch, rather than that black-and-white flatlander, the lark bunting, deserves to be Colorado's state bird.

The brown-capped rosy finch, rare in distribution but hardy on home ground, is so far unthreatened by the follies of mankind. Its identity for birders, however, is menaced by the taxonomists. Because of hybridization between overlapping species of rosy finches, and uncertainty over whether isolated species of rosy finches could interbreed if they did collide, there is speculation that the rosy finch species of North America may be simply a single species of bird, with local variation. It is possible, for instance, that as the glaciers receded, isolated groups of rosy finches may have become stranded in their alpine fastnesses, to diverge slightly in behavior and coloration. One cannot help being reminded of another group of nearly identical finches — the ones on the Galapagos Islands that led Darwin to such productive thinking on the mechanism of biological evolution. When more is known, the American Ornithologists' Union, which passes on such matters, may decree that the North American rosy finches are merely local varieties, or races, of a single generic rosy finch. While the bird may not object, it would be distinctly bad news to the thousands of birders who have traveled to Colorado to rack up our alpine exclusive. The Colorado Chamber of Commerce, in the name of potential lost revenues, should be ready to protest.

But a rosy finch by any other name is still our optimistic little bird, worthy of a few well-focused moments on your next major ascent. To the degree that birdlife honors human borders, the brown capped rosy finch, modest though it may be, is very much our own.

10.

Lunch!

What ties up the Aspen phone system every day from mid-morning until noon? What do Aspenites scream at each other from opposite ends of the mall when the sun approaches meridian? What do some fanatics line up a week in advance? What enriches an eighth of the population and bankrupts the rest? What, after tourism and construction, is Aspen's greatest industry? Ah, but you've peeked at the title. . . .

Nourishment is the least by-product. One can get through the noon meal more easily at home, or out of a paper bag, or by ignoring it altogether. Even the excuse of checking out a new restaurant or sampling a new dish is a gastronomic façade. Ritualized eating is one of the achievements of our species, and our midday jaws are often more primed for speech than mastication. Man is a pack animal and lunch, at its most mythic level, is secular communion, a rite of tribal bonding. How can any day be considered wasted which includes lunch?

The crowd I've fallen in with drifts in and out of town in a pattern that roughly correlates with an absence of snow. Our convergence, never quite planned, is the opposite of winter, and is known as the Luncheon Season. During that spell we leave no old classic unvisited, and no new effort unsampled lest it vanish by the next snowfall. When one of our number feels the day is ripe, he or she will scream the magic word over the phone, or merely grunt like a peccary. We will gather before noon to have our pick of tables, and linger until three, or until the glare of personnel can no longer be withstood. So many variables shape those magic hours — our own humors and personalities, the situation of the table, the tolerance of the waiter or waitress, even the food — that what might lapse into habit is constantly charged with the unforeseen.

Devotion to the public trough generates a private folklore. Now legendary, for instance, is the most inspired Mexican cooking ever to hit the mall, a few tables whose name we breathed in everyone's face for weeks and which nonetheless folded by Labor Day. Superlatives have included Salad Niçoise at The Tippler, Chicken Julienne at Ute City Banque, omelette #4 at the original Andre's and spinach enchiladas at DiMaggio's in Basalt. But perfect lunches, those noontides when good food, company and service come seamlessly together, are, so to speak, self-consuming — intensely enjoyed at the moment, beyond recall a week later. Tolstoy's dictum about families could be extended: all happy lunches are alike, but every unhappy lunch is unhappy in its own way. Thanks to the perversity of human nature, it is the disasters that live in our hearts.

Which among us will ever forget our long-awaited sampling of the successful restaurant that moved across the street into a multi-story format with a private disco upstairs, and appointments rumored to cost in the hundred of thousands. . . . On the way in we glanced at a chalkboard on the sidewalk proclaiming, Today's Special — Grilled Vegetarian. "What a terrible thing to do to those nice people who don't eat meat," murmured Abigail, as if savoring the possibilities. We took our choice of tables, being the first customers, and Pierre, ever the adventurer, ordered the buffalo burger with mountain fries. What arrived sometime later, marooned with two French fries on a vast white platter, was a patty of tough ground meat on a parched bun, looking vaguely like a pygmy in an Elizabethan collar. Pierre eyed it with hostility, ventured a bite, swallowed with some deliberation and much water. He asked the waiter if he couldn't bring something to help it along. After an impressive lapse the waiter, with a theatrical flourish, produced a thin slice of tomato and one more fry. Pierre concluded, in retrospect, that it was the contrast between the waiter's self-righteous generosity in offering the tomato and supplemental fry, and the rigors of downing the buffalo chip without the least lubricant of mayonnaise, that so tattooed the meal on his psyche.

Equally historic was a debacle in one of the operations attempted in the space now occupied by the successful Little Annie's, though whether it was The Roman Lion, Car 19 or the French number, I no longer recall. Again the place was empty, and to conserve the effect the waitress escorted us to the farthest and darkest booth. It wasn't until our pupils dilated that we found the benches and tablecloth deep in shards of the previous meal. We rashly ordered, then the waitress returned to inform us they were out of those items. We ordered again, confirming availability, and decided a bottle of wine might be advisable. Could the waitress recommend something light and dry, a Rhine perhaps or a Moselle? The waitress didn't know much about wines but would check. She returned after a hotly debated silence. "Yes," she beamed, "we do have a fine Löwenbräu..."

On a scale of four stars some restaurants rate a black hole, and mercifully implode. More problematical are the decent places one can no longer take because The Music Is Too Loud or Paul Harvey holds court over the radio. There are corner-cutters, like the atrium that runs out of their turkey special of Thanksgiving proportions and tries to palm off pressed turkey over sandwich bread, but one complains at one's risk. A friend remained loyal to a leading Aspen institution despite years of decline, and finally bit into a chicken-fried steak that seemed tainted. He summoned the waitress, who apologized profusely and took it back to the kitchen. Twenty-five minutes later she brought back the same piece of meat with its missing bite and announced brightly, "The chef says it's okay." A year later the customer, unflinchingly loyal, beckoned the owner. "I hate to say this," he said, "but I'm afraid your food recently has really been going downhill."

"Was that Wednesday?" shot back the owner. "I was in Glenwood."

Saddest in my experience is the terrace under the parachute silk, where for two decades Aspenites and visitors lingered over civilized conversation and the world's most celestial omelettes. No matter that the place fell to Americans, that the omelettes were newly leavened with concrete and the croissants became dinner rolls in crescent drag. One could still admire the clematis and exchange thoughts like a human being, and in that spirit I suggested the place to a friend with whom I had a year's worth of catching up. We dispatched the requisite food, and the waitress was kind enough to keep asking if we wanted something else. No, well perhaps a tad more coffee. At last the hostess came over and asked us to leave: with us sitting there like that, how could they turn over the table? We obliged, permanently.

But the award-winning Bad Lunch story was snared by Army Armstrong, who with his wife Sara began his own lunch place in the mid-Fifties and turned it into the Copper Kettle, one of Aspen's — and America's — great restaurants. Always interested in his colleagues, Army decided to try a lunch place in what was once a bowling alley, is now Fothergill Sports, and for a week had been a burger-and-sausage counter called Der Wurst Place. In the classic manner of the tragic lunch hero Army was first to arrive, and ordered his hamburger. The young chef slapped it on the grill, and the chef's girl friend clumped in complaining that her ski boots were so cold they were killing her. "Take them off," ordered the chef. The girl did, and handed them to the chef, who placed them on the grill. Army, normally taciturn, observed the tongue of mud and snow licking toward his lunch. "I'm sorry," he intruded, "but that's really unsanitary."

The chef drew himself to his full height, leaned forward, looked Army in the eye and with the full weight of his week as a restauranteur replied, "You know, it's people like you who are ruining Aspen."

So indelible is the exquisitely bad lunch that unmemorable good lunches, which abound by comparison, often consist in comparing past calamities. If there is no such thing as a free lunch, over the long haul there is no such thing as the bad lunch one survives. In fact the mystique may not have to surround lunch at all, and in a faster crowd, a similar halo may envelop dinner. But such are evening prices that I seldom find myself going public with other locals; when I dine out it is generally with visitors, and it is principally other visitors I see. Breakfast, of course, may be hilarious for those who eat it.

To every domain there is surely a favored occasion. In London it may be tiffin, and in Florence Junction it may be a moonlit gathering of peccaries around an uprooted yucca. In Pitkin County, like platinum awaiting its ruby, lies gastronomic high noon. The sky will blacken and the earth revolve before the opportunity returns. There are only so many lunches in your life. Call someone.

11.

Confessions of a Chef Salad Eater

The best way to have your cake and eat it too is to order a chef salad. One eats and eats, yet the salad is not consumed — nor does one fill up. High on nutrition, low on calories, bristling with roughage, sufficiently varied that one bite does not determine the next, chef salads are an elegant way to survive. They leave the addict refreshed, recharged, and just a little smug.

Of course, some salads are more transcendent than others. The minimal offering consists of chopped iceberg (or head) lettuce with slivered ham and American cheese, half a hardboiled egg, a quartered tomato and a cellophane packet with two crackers. Iceberg lettuce has the least flavor and food value of all greens, the ham may be fatty, and American cheese is chronically a flat, processed ochre, but if that is their salad you are still smart to have eschewed their hamburger.

Joy, as always, enters with variety. Ordering a chef, I have been issued chicken, turkey, salami, roast beef rare and smoked, radishes, raw onions, cherry tomatoes, mushrooms, jalapeño peppers, taco chips, kidney and garbanzo beans, sliced oranges, black olives, Swiss cheese, feta, raw carrot, cucumber, zucchini, red cabbage, green pepper, and much unidentified foliage. Also alfalfa sprouts, a hip new legume whose cool crunchiness leaves, at least in this palate, a nasty kicker. But remove what you don't like — that's what the ashtray is for — and eat in the assurance that the chef has not been required to cook and can have done your lunch no damage. Out of the hundreds of chef salads I have dispatched, I only choked at one. The lettuce was rotten, served with a snarl, and was truly the salad of the bad café.

Ordering a salad you are faced with one option: the dressing. The classic complement to lettuce, moistening and heightening it without clobbering the flavor, is vinegar and oil, served in separate flagons so you can ration your own. If it comes pre-mixed you will have to trust the chef with the vinegar. When I grew up that combination was called French dressing. So it remained into the mid-Sixties, when I spent several ascetic years in Spain, a realm where vinegar and oil of the olive is *all* one puts on salad. When I returned to New York and ordered French dressing in a Seventh Avenue lunchette, the owner offered to whip some up if I didn't mind the wait. Fifteen minutes later the salad emerged under a sweet magma of tomato, for which I expressed a quite mystified and insincere gratitude. Pre-mixed vinegar and oil, I later learned, is *Italian* dressing. In America, then, it becomes a litany: one asks for vinegar and oil, is advised there is Italian, and gets anything from polluted mayonnaise to cream garlic. In luck one will stumble on some inventive house creation — vinegar and oil with curious herbs, or a biting lemon oil — or the classic two vials. You are always at liberty to order the Roquefort or the bleu cheese or the green goddess or plain mayo, but that will reduce all variety to the same molasses, you will get fat, and you might as well have ordered the Reuben.

Ordering, of course, is elementary; the art is in the eating. Ideally the ingredients will arrive mixed, or served on a plate large enough that you can cut and mix them yourself. But most chefs resent the time it takes to cut up all those bitty items and arrange them with Euclidian flash in the bowl, and take revenge by making the salad as difficult to eat as possible — and, I sense, by instructing the server not to ask how your salad is until your mouth is full and you can only grunt. The most sadistic instance I know of is served in a chain restaurant in Phoenix, and is called a Rainforest Retreat. The bowl is perhaps five inches across, slick as greased linoleum, and from its

Rainforest Retreat

Jalapeno Pepper

carefully cantilevered very sturdy Romaine

five inch bowl

sides portend three great leaves of romaine which double the bowl's diameter, heaped to the tip with chopped iceberg, cheese, ham, turkey, green onion, a carrot stick, a radish rosette and a hard-boiled egg. To reduce the problem I first eat the carrot, the radish, and the egg, and lay the onion on the table. Taking the knife and fork, I fold the romaine inward and sever the tips into the other ingredients. I sliver the green onion into the mix, wield the oil and vinegar and commence to eat my way down, slicing into it more romaine as the level subsides and the brew homogenizes. Half my lunch winds up on the table, but I figure, hell, they served it, they can clean it up.

The disposal of a chef salad is, in fact, quite antisocial, and in delicate company you are better off with the quiche. But if you are lunching alone, at table or booth, you might as well make it a bravura performance and read the news at the same time — not some niggling little tabloid like the *Rocky Mountain News* or the *Aspen Times,* but a genuine 24 by 28-incher like the *Denver Post.* In Aspen you can perform the further feat of trying to screen out Paul Harvey. Since the cholesterol is low, you will not aggravate the heart attack surely lurking among the editorials. Let the pages turn, let the ham and lettuce fly, and wash it all down with strong black coffee. Heart racing, palate ringing, well-nourished, moderately informed, smug but not overstuffed — you are ready to assault the afternoon.

12.

Notes of a Half-Aspenite II

Certain dry spirits find snow on the ground about as interesting as snow on TV. Their idea of a perfect day at sea may be to lie in the desert reading Conrad, and as Aspenites they may head for dry ground when their homes lie under water whipped into flakes. Fire signs in exile, they forgive the white-out knowing that Aspen will bloom again, deciduous and artistic. If obsessive enough to keep journals, they may even rifle back pages like these.

Aspen, reputed to Have Everything, is rather poor in chronology, and none will be imposed on the following.

August 14, 1977

We were seated cross-legged on Persian carpets, staring at a low table with brassy place settings that suggested dinner. The calm was uncanny. At last a waiter glided up. We ordered drinks and appetizers. The waiter sank from sight. A few more diners arrived. We sent a busboy to pry the waiter forth. He appeared with the wrong drinks, apologized, and after a mysterious interval returned with new drinks.

"The appetizers?" someone suggested.

"Oh, certainly."

By the time we finished the drinks he returned with taboulli instead of stuffed grape leaves. At this point taboulli was just fine; could we order dinner? He drifted to the kitchen with our order and, perhaps, continued down the coal chute. The more recent arrivals had already been served their kabob by an efficient waitress; could she exhume our waiter? He floated back empty-handed. "We have been here an hour and a half," stated our spokesperson, "and you haven't got anything right. What *is* going on?" The waiter burst into tears.

Suddenly we felt alarmed, even protective. What was wrong? Could we do anything to help?

"You'll have to forgive me," he sobbed. "This is my first acid trip."

August 4, 1978

Went to the jeweler to get my watch cleaned. A local shopkeeper came in with a shoe in his hand and asked the jeweler to repair the ornamental buckle. The jeweler scowled at the loafer. "I'm afraid I only work in silver and gold," he breathed, implying a certain baseness about the buckle.

"But what can I do?" pleaded the customer. "I can only replace this shoe in New York."

"Well," said the jeweler sadly, "I've seen a kid with a torch working on junk in the Brand Building. . . ."

July 31, 1985

As the latest piece of shingled bloat plugs one of the last streets with a view into space, it's been a pleasure to watch the construction crew nail the roof with crosses as if warding off the vampires of taste. Pierre and I toured the exterior, prowled inside in quest of Interesting Spaces, then asked a man laying flagstones about some unaccountable projecting second-story rooms without floors. "I just do my job," he said, "I don't look up." Over his head stretched a faded banner: OPENING SOON! 31 FLAVORS.

June 23, 1984

Last night just before I went to bed I heard the garbage can rattle. The culprit, at last! I ran screaming out to nab him, froze, then backed off cooing, "Nice kitty, sweet kitty, such a clever white stripe down your back. . ."

June 30, 1986

Am revising my opinion of the shingled bloat. During my absence the façade has been plastered with sandstone blocks so small they are clearly non-structural, making real stone look fake. A jutting doorway of the same cubes — a joke arch or an arch joke — adds a grade school stage effect. Now the driveway has been reddened to throw a rose blush on one side of the house, making the real-into-fake stones look unmatched. Could anything short of lawn flamingoes improve this postmodern kitsch? Reality, that wit, came up with two; an architectural award and a For Sale sign.

July 14, 1982

Must learn to leave messages without fright on phone recording machines. I arranged with my piano teacher that I would leave a characteristic sound instead of my voice, and next time I got his recorded message I struck the gong he knows so well. Later I ran into him and accused him of not returning the call. As we reconstructed it, I struck the gong before the system began to record, all he got was the dying reverberation, and he took it for some crank flushing the toilet.

August 3, 1979

The young man sat in the front window of the *Aspen Times,* gazed moodily at the oncoming storm, and observed, "This is my favorite kind of weather, ideal for wearing a corduroy jacket with pigskin trimming."

November 7, 1984

Spent nearly an hour trying to peel, scratch, and razor the bumper sticker off my car. Mondale flaked right off but Ferraro hung tough.

July 2, 1974

Dennis wanted to try out his new two-man inflatable raft: did I know any stretch where we could float a couple of miles and savor the view? I wasn't too familiar with the streams but thought we could put in at Difficult Campground and drift to town. Most of it you could see from the road, and looked so sluggish you'd probably have to paddle to move at all.

We blew up the raft and launched ourselves from the parking lot. The raft swung luxuriously past the fishermen, around the first bend and to the brink of the foaming throat of a mad dog. We swung and plunged, our pulse hemorrhaged, and I thought briefly of the sniper scene in *Deliverance*. We grabbed a granite boulder mid-cascade and clung with all our adrenaline. Now what? We screamed a plan, and pushed simultaneously toward the nearest shore with just enough propulsion to grab the tips of some willows. Shaking, we portaged back to the parking lot after a bracing three-minute ride.

July 17, 1972

Love gossiping about Aspen in Spanish with Sigfrido, partly because he translates even the names of the local establishments. The Hotel Jerome, for instance, becomes *El Hotel Jerónimo,* while the Red Onion is *La Cebolla Roja.* But last night when he mentioned a boarding house called *Las Noches* I was stumped. Did the place have a Spanish title, or was he referring to something called The Nights? *"No,"* he explained patiently, *"es la cabina de dos pisos al lado del lift uno, tu la conoces bien."*

I thought hard, then it burst upon me. *"Claro. La* Snowchase!"

June 30, 1983

In the bathroom under Clark's Market, instead of paper towels there is one of those energy-gobbling hot-air hand dryers with careful instructions:

1. Push Button
2. Rub Hands Gently Under Warm Air.
3. Stops Automatically.

Someone else must have had the same trouble adapting, for a printed tape underneath adds:

4. Wipe Hands On Pants.

June 30, 1976

A neighbor called to say her toothbrush was flopping around the sink and wouldn't stop. Club it on the snout, I suggested. Come quickly, she implored. Turned out to be a battery operated model that made my whole arm sizzle before I got the switch unstuck.

October 3, 1985

Was swimming laps at the Snowmass Club when a riderless bicycle materialized on the berm beyond the pool and coasted across my field of vision more steady than any human being could have held it. What had launched it? Why didn't it tip over? Was my guest card good for visions? At last the bicycle veered miraculously into the sky, disclosing beneath it the truck that was bearing it toward Highline Road.

70

November 15, 1985

Daily physical therapy at the Snowmass Club has yielded a few more surprises. Just beyond the athletic club door I found two roses lying on the sidewalk in the season's first snow. I picked them up: just short of full bloom, they had been cut correctly on the diagonal, close as if for insertion in lapels, and radiated one of those unnamable shades between orange and pink, as if they'd been sculpted from smoked salmon. I placed them in liqueur glasses on my windowsill and watched them gradually unfold until, two afternoons later, the sun came out unexpectedly and nuked them.

A week later the man swimming laps so professionally in the next lane stopped at the end of the pool, lifted his goggles, and studied the snowy berm in fascination. I stopped too. "Look!" he whispered, "a fox." Given my eyesight without glasses I wouldn't have known the creature from a dachshund, but I fingered back the skin over my left eyelid until I got the animal in shaky focus. It was lustrous and bushy-tailed; advanced, backtracked, then rose straight in the air and pounced. "Got its meal," breathed my companion. We resumed our laps gingerly, scanning the snow.

There was jacuzzi repartee: "I always come to Snowmass in the fall to lose weight."

"Why's that?"

"There's no place to eat."

"That's because Snowmass is a four-season resort. Two on and two off."

Once I sat in the jacuzzi with a burly type of Nordic coloration, a no-nonsense demeanor, and a florid tattoo over his heartside pectoral, an array of shamrock and hibiscus framing a slanted inscription lost to my poor vision — nor did it seem wise to stare while drawing back my eyelid. But I had to know: was it Betty? Mom? Jesse Helms? I snared it while climbing out: it said "Aspen."

June 14, 1980

How resourceful of the hostess to ensure a vegetarian meal by preparing the main course herself and asking a carnivorous guest to bring the salad. And how resourceful of the guest to supply a taco salad, brimming with spiced ground beef.

October 16, 1981

A playing card lay face down on the sidewalk in front of Tom's Market. "Call it," I said.

"Nine of spades," said Bobby.

"Three of diamonds," said I.

It was the joker.

May 16, 1985

Although it's Thursday, all the businesses in The Hague are closed for Ascension Day, and the streets are calm as pedestrian malls. I stopped by some pools under chestnut trees by a row of embassies. Low branches cut off the view overhead, but one could see the great trunks blooming downward through a scrim of dust on the still water, and the surrounding billows of fresh leaves, wide as the hands of Rachmaninoff, receding through fathoms of green cut glass. Into these depths a pair of black and white silhouettes swooped, flitted, skirmished, shook the submerged boughs, and roiled the deep waters while shrieking in counterpoint overhead. I had never seen magpies upside down before, but through all this lushness I could suddenly smell the dust, and fill my ribcage with thin, exhilarating air. Soon I would be seeing these birds rightside up, in my own yard.

13.

My Yard Is Between Things

When I was lucky enough to find an affordable house in Aspen, it came with an acre of land and a full spectrum of terrain. Attention first plunges one hundred feet to the creek, then out to the peaks that constitute the View. Sated, one discovers the stand of cottonwoods laced with spruce saplings, Rocky Mountain maples, man-sized dogwoods and assorted verdure that filters traffic, deadens the noon whistle and gives a sense of withdrawal from town. Only gradually does one find the lawn full of high-altitude grasses, weeds and wildflowers; a relict population of the sage that preceded persons and trees; the slope of chokecherries, serviceberries and mountain alders that falls to water. And the area adjacent to the house was cursed, upon my arrival, with iris, Oriental poppies, peonies, privet and delphinium.

Cursed? The flowers, in fact, recall the best feature of the Chicago suburb where I grew up — its flora — and iris in its wilder strain remains my favorite flower. But such foliage, heir to centuries of cross-breeding, spadework and thought, needs further floriculture to survive. The couple who built the house in the late Forties spent twenty years preparing flower beds, fertilizing peonies and poppies, separating iris bulbs and watering it all on cue. Now, by deed of transfer, their charges were thrust on my mercy.

Looking back far enough I could locate in myself the gardening impulse, and during kindergarten and the early grades I attempted that contradiction in terms, a wildflower garden. Hauling a toy wagon to every vacant lot, I dug up all the wild geraniums, jack-in-the-pulpits and trilliums within a mile radius and planted them under the pines by the garage, where most of them died. As an angel of death I was only a few years ahead of the bulldozer, and enough survived that I dashed home daily from school, dodging bullies through the alleys, to see who had grown a new leaf, or even bloomed. Every plant was as full of feeling as myself or our spaniel, and far more so than my schoolmates.

At that time I wanted to be a florist if I couldn't be a dancer, though I knew a greenhouse would condemn me to a lifetime of poinsettias, gladiolas and mums. Those were the tame and less feeling plants with the huge fake blooms, so strangely favored by adults. They took root only in pure dirt, and anything that sprang up next to them was a weed and got pulled; like school bullies, they owned the turf. Siding with the floral underdog became my undoing when my mother, knowing I liked to handle plants, asked me to help weed the vegetables. I tried to please her, but as I pulled the stems I could feel the roots clinging desperately to the earth, hauling bits of it with them as I tore friends from their homes and tossed them in a limp pile, where they turned pale and died in the sun. My mother, seeing her neurotic child couldn't be trusted to eliminate the rag-weed between two rows of beans, said, "It's all right to pull them — they don't have feelings, you know." The parental voice must have out-ranked fraternal feeling, for at that moment something in me snapped and the entire vegetable kingdom — as brotherhood rather than object of admiration — died. If I couldn't become a dancer, I would raise dogs.

It was with a certain psychic residue, then, that in my late twenties I acquired, along with the house, the Russells' flower garden. As providers of living color I wished the plants well. I realized that if I didn't tend them I would turn my back on twenty years of previous devotion, and I thought of the Russells with guilt. But to care for them properly would keep me as rooted as they were. Some childhood sympathy kept me from hauling them out bodily, so I struck a Darwinian compromise: I would let all fellow inhabitants grow naturally, water and fertilize the lawn, clip the bushes, and wouldn't coddle the exotics. It was an ultimatum: make it or mulch it. My own punishment would be to watch the yard, once featured on the Aspen Home and Garden Tour, keep trying without me.

The peonies gave up first. Their bed lay just outside the door, where my German shepherd performed his circle dance in anticipation of our walks, and he took care of each year's sprouts while the lawn overcame the bed like a slow tide. The delphinium shrank into caricatures of the larkspur they derived from. The iris gave up blooming, the bulbs no doubt a single tuberous mass, though they persisted in sending up pathetic green spikes. The poppies made an annual ferny heap under the lilacs, sent up stems weighty with promise, then blanched and collapsed before they could flower. The poppies did have a remission the year it was popular to talk to plants. One night, propelled by the third scotch and thinking to undo the moment in the bean garden, I crawled under the lilacs and explained, at my florid best, the zen of blooming. To my alarm, a couple of days later the poppies unfurled two gorgeous scarlet blossoms. But pep talks in subsequent years produced nothing, one year they bloomed without advice, and the evidence is inconclusive.

If the heirs of breeding died in their beds, the wild rabble rushed in, particularly on the lawn. The grass, itself a strain rustled from a higher valley, was increasingly colonized by penstemon, paintbrush, salsify, clover, yarrow, and other grasses, spiked here with aspen saplings, there leafed out with dandelions. It is a joy to watch each snowmelt unveil its riot of surprises. During the summer I fertilize with anything free of weed killer, cut selectively with a scythe, and at its best the lawn has the sculpted look of a razor cut. The taste for the one-plant lawn has always baffled me, and it is my ultimate hope that the grass will, in some nicely textured way, phase itself out.

Fortunately my eccentric lawn is tucked away in back, safe from scorn, while what passes for a front yard is a vestige of the sage, wildflowers and old boilers that once stretched from my house to the bridge into town. I relished the way my yard melted into it with no visible property line — until I learned that what wasn't mine was to be cleared for a condominium complex. Hoping to head off any incursion I met with the developer. He assured me his crew would respect the line, that I could order partitioning trees through him at half price, and that he would spare all possible native vegetation on his own side. He tossed his filter tip into the irrigation stream and we shook on it.

The dozers arrived and cleared all but the tallest cottonwoods. I positioned a stepladder at my property's edge. It was quickly felled. I approached the foreman to request a new ladder, to ask that the line be respected and to place an order for some trees, and was informed that the developer had left no instructions and could not be reached. The completed project looked like kids' dressers from the unpainted furniture store, became known locally as Chateau Caca, and a sadistic friend suggested a twenty-foot fence with a mirror facing the Chateau. Not wanting to alienate several dozen innocent new neighbors, I settled for a bevy of young spruce, at full price. Subsequent summers I could be seen wielding the hose as never before, and giving them the old poppy talk: grow, siblings, grow.

Letting my terrain become God's little acre might seem blame-less enough if pieces of it didn't keep blowing onto the more elegant spread of my horsey neighbor, Local Velvet. Through the cotton-woods I could see it all shimmer: the beds of delphinium, columbine and Shasta daisies, the glitter of sprinklers, the monocultural lawn like a sporty par 3. It is hardly my fault that prevailing winds carry my dandelion, salsify and cottonwood seeds, dead leaves and backwater mosquitoes into Eden. Nor was it my doing that the magpies in my cottonwoods ate the suet for Miss Velvet's orioles and pecked at her horses. Order itself, I tend to think, is a small clearing in the larger disorder, and is made more delicious by a howling over the fence.

But exactly what is that howling? From the degenerate side of the fence it is nothing more than letting dandelions flourish where they land, magpies build where they will, allowing one thing to happen when you might have expected another. It is the spectacle of a German shepherd helping high-altitude grasses take over from low-altitude peonies, the pleasure of watching wild roses ace out the privet. By Judeo-Christian tradition it is synonymous with moral abdication, darkness, all we were cursed with when we were kicked out of the Garden; Krishna would more likely have called it detachment. By whatever name, it is the very chaos that evolved these fine brains that pronounce judgment on chaos itself. Encoded in all this hemlock and ragweed is an order more vast than our cleverness can unravel. It spawned us and survives within us. It is, as Henry James might say, the figure in the carpet.

A few years ago my largest cottonwood was felled by a spring storm. For two years it produced no leaves, and I had left it because I liked the thickness of the trunk, the way it marked the end of the lawn, and because every evening a flock of cedar waxwings lit in the crown to roost, turning it into a living candelabra. I had clearly overplayed my detachment by letting it stand, and was lucky that it fell cleanly, missing the house and other trees, barely nicking Miss Velvet's fence. Now that it was down it somehow completed the forest, and I decided to let it rot in style.

Miss Velvet, leaning over the nick, remarked that the sight of the fallen giant made her sad, and to leave it that way seemed downright morbid. Besides, she added with a sly gleam, it would make splendid firewood if it were chopped in time. I had my own definitions of morbidity but I did need firewood. I ran into the tree surgeon downtown, and on impulse I asked him to chainsaw it into sections so I could split it from there. I borrowed a sledge and wedge, began to split the tree with visions of cord upon cord, and triggered a spinal misalignment from which I am still recovering. The remainder of the tree still rots, not in style but in random cylinders that look, to their betrayer, like ill-stacked vertebrae.

There are limits, perhaps here surpassed, to seeing nature as parable or psychic identification. I confess to loving not only native plants but the exotics that *didn't* mulch it — including lilacs, crabapples, clematis, woodbine, silver maple, Norwegian spruce, hops and lily-of-the-valley. I keenly miss the little Russian olive that danced in the wind like a young figure skater, lost to a June freeze. And so protective have I become of my chaos that I nearly called the cops on some strangers' horses tethered to my cottonwoods after a parade, eating my chaos to the roots. Every Fourth of July I now tack up cardboards proclaiming independence for the weeds, and a sawhorse that warns NO HORSES BUT THIS ONE.

Protected randomness may be as much of a contradiction as my first wildflower garden, and to a stranger's eye it may not look natural, just messy. I haven't found the pattern myself and am prepared to explain, if pressed, that my yard is between things. It's a safe evasion. The figure in the carpet is always changing and we are all, at every moment, between things.

14.

Open House

The whole thrust of domestic architecture, from mud huts through the industrial revolution, has been to keep nature out of the house. In the main we have succeeded. We can correct weather with a spin of the dial, are no longer menaced by bears in our bedrooms, and the structures themselves are impervious to all but floods, fires, and the highway commission. But by evolutionary standards human shelter is a novelty, and entire classes of creatures that thrive under cover now share our notions of the dream house. Mice, earwigs, pack rats, moths, silverfish: one need only name a few species to make the point. Many of these creatures have gone through several generations before the legal owners even move in. Consciously or not, every householder has to decide whether to tolerate these guests or do them in.

It was certainly no surprise when the house I bought in Aspen in 1968 turned out to have been colonized by two decades of pack rats, mice, insects, and human beings. The pack rats, I was told, had survived every manner of trap and poison, but never descended from the crawl space between the ceiling and the roof. The insects and mice would be sharing ground level. As the new human being, I hoped to avoid a confrontation.

The pack rats, as promised, never left the crawl space — an area I didn't much care for — and fell silent whenever my fist on the ceiling disturbed their nocturnal Olympics; there seemed little point to a search-and-destroy mission doomed to failure. The mice behaved badly in ways that needn't elaboration, and would have to be dealt with. What most struck me was that with every new burst of sunshine, in midsummer or the depths of February, fresh crops of insects would erupt from the rug as if by spontaneous generation, to fling their hopeless lives against the glass on their way to the light. Outside, by contrast, there were hardly any insects at all, and the wind over Castle Creek blew away even the mosquitoes. What, then, was the point of all these screens that made you open two doors to get out, that covered the windows like a fine-mesh jail? Were they keeping the flies out or in? Against the advice of a solicitous neighbor who warned me of invasions of fauna I still haven't seen, I unhinged all that ill-smelling, light-deadening wire and chucked it into permanent storage.

Of the few inappropriate creatures to cross the threshold since, the majority have been birds. For the birds it is an inconvenience; for the novice birder it is a gift. Birds generally head for the nearest closed window, where they are easily caught by maneuvering them against a corner of the frame, slipping a brandy snifter over them, sliding a shirt cardboard between the snifter and the pane, and trapping them in a connoisseur's bell jar. If they are colorfully marked, they get held to the light, and if they are a new species they are matched with entries in the bird book before they are dismissed. I first identified a MacGillivray's warbler in my bedroom: how but in the hand, rather than the bush, could I have told a bird best distinguished from lookalikes by a broken eye ring?

In fourteen years my open door policy has been abused only twice by vertebrates, both drawn by the lure of the sea. A stray housecat, weary of trimming the songbird population, once leapt on top of my refrigerator and shredded an ingot of frozen fish I had left to defrost before I hissed into sight. More calamitous was a magpie that attacked the shell collection along my inner sill while an enraged sidekick tried to help from outside by jabbing the glass. My yells went ignored and, amid shattered sand dollars and trepanned pelican skulls, I was forced to pull the brandy snifter trick with a wicker wastebasket and a slim art book, then throw basket, book, and bird out the door in a burst of mauled possessions and lost feathers.

A house, with or without screens, mocks in a squarish way forms already found in nature; it is miraculous, deceitful glass for which evolution is unprepared. No matter how dirty you keep your windows, birds will still brain themselves on the illusion of sky. But glass can be more playful. I was once almost nose to beak with a red-tailed hawk perched on a scrub oak outside, more likely staring at its own reflection or the mirrored beyond than at myself. At the same window, during an inhouse insect bloom, a large fly batted itself against a window bottom while a hypnotized Wilson's warbler, a fixation of shrill yellow, hopped outside trying to feast through the pane.

If we could project ourselves into another species' brain, it would be particularly curious to follow the disruptions we make in their worldview. What does a magpie think when its companion is demolishing sand dollars while all it strikes is a cold, odorless wall? What does the warbler make of the fly it can chase but can't sniff or eat? I have played my wolf and whale records for my German shepherd; he briefly cocked his head when the speaker yelped, but whales were about as interesting as the Chicago Symphony. Do animals take our tricks seriously? Report miracles? Go mad? They never tell us, but a safe guess is that they drop the matter and proceed to firm ground.

Whether a homeowner enjoys playing host species to assorted rabble is probably a matter of temperament. I am personally entertained by a cortège of red ants shouldering a dead bee along the windowsill; in my own home I am probably as close as I will come to a sense of life on other worlds. I admire the way spiders lace up my old bottle collection, and there is even practical value in having some odd little friends to speed the phobic houseguest on his way. It is less stimulating when a mouse dies a pungent and inaccessible death behind the refrigerator just as renters are due, and efforts to sweeten the situation only smell like someone died in a pine tree. A friend, horrified to see me finally resorting to traps, left a note for the mice: "The owner of this house is plotting against you. Beware of certain devices baited with cheese. When the cheese is disturbed, a coiled bar will descend, perhaps fatally. Flee while you can." The note included a detailed diagram of the trap.

"Do you really think the mice are literate?" I asked.

"No, but they'll get the vibration."

I am forced to report that no mice were killed, or even seen, for the remainder of the season.

There are certain risks in a house without screens, without poisons, where the flower arrangements have real bees, and where your reluctant traps are sabotaged by still more faint-hearted friends. But risk is not boredom, and the glass is more miraculous when it gives back more life than your own inhospitable face.

15.

Perils of the Visiting Writer

One of the better fringe benefits of life in Aspen is that one can be thrown into contact with the famous and fascinating without being anyone in particular oneself. As a celebrity trap Aspen especially favored the editors of *Aspen Anthology*, a ruthlessly non-profit literary magazine with a token national circulation. Under various names, the journal was kept from extinction through the Seventies and early Eighties by a band of floating literati. What we needed to give circulation a boost, we figured, were a few familiar names in our pages — names whose owners were unlikely to trade a profitable manuscript for two copies of the magazine. Our only way to publish them gratis was to trap them bodily when they showed up in Aspen for a conference and hope they wouldn't risk offending the locals by refusing an interview.

But our office was a bit cramped for grilling strangers. It seemed impolite to invade their temporary quarters, and our own preferred venue — the Jerome Bar — might strike them as unserious. Aspen does have its own well-known, well-housed authors, but they kept their distance from our scene, even as their houses tend to look down on the town. *Aspen Anthology's* editors, on the other hand, typically camped in basements, in disheveled flats, or on other people's sofas. By process of elimination, my house was our best alternative, and I was privileged to play host, briefly, to luminaries I would otherwise have encountered only on the page.

Our first victim was Tom Wolfe, in town for the 1976 Aspen Design Conference. On opening morning he gave a talk characterizing the Seventies as the Me Decade, then the conference broke for lunch. We thought we too had time for lunch, and slipped to the Jerome Bar for a sandwich and beer. We returned to the Conference tent ten minutes late for our appointment to transport Wolfe to the interview, and he was nowhere to be found. In a mild panic, we trotted around the canvas and the Conference displays, then took off, panting, through the vegetational geometries of the Aspen Institute, making cracks about Wolfe hunts. We brought our quarry to bay just before he regained his apartment at the Aspen Meadows and herded him back to my jeep. I had forgotten that Wolfe wears only the white, three-piece suits he calls one of his two greatest pleasures in life, and I was hotly aware of the caked mud on the passenger seat.

Waiting to ambush Wolfe in my living room was Aspen sculptress Missy Thorne, whom Wolfe had satirized in *Radical Chic*, his send-up of a fashionable party Leonard Bernstein had thrown for the Black Panthers. Introducing Thorne, Wolfe had written, "A beautiful ash-blond girl with the most perfect Miss Porter's face speaks up. She's wearing a leather and tweed dress. She looks like a Junior Leaguer graduating to the Ungaro Boutique." Throughout the piece, Ash Blond appears as the naive young socialite in over her depth. When *Radical Chic* was published, Thorne had written to Wolfe to complain that he had used the occasion to take cheap shots when he might have used his position to shed light on the Black Panthers, signing herself Ash Blond. It was with trepidation, then, that I introduced Wolfe to Miss Thorne, who smiled icily and replied, "I'm Ash Blond."

"Then why didn't you sign your name to the letter?" he shot back.

There was a pause when I thought the stuff of lawsuits might ensue, then Missy confessed that she, like he, had never met the Bernsteins and had also crashed the party out of curiosity. Revealed as partners in crime, they began laughing about the Bernstein affair like old cronies, and the flare-up left us all more at ease.

Throughout the interview Wolfe defended his good spirits in the face of world crisis, almost anticipating questions with his pixie-like Virginia charm, and at last excused himself to the bathroom. I suddenly remembered that the john had been backing up at irregular intervals and spilling onto the floor, while my plumber was spending the week in seclusion. There was a flush, then a long wait while I listened for clues over editorial chatter. Wolfe emerged saying that the bowl had spilled over, that he had done the best he could to mop it up with toilet paper, and that he hoped there was no damage to the floor. The floor was beyond damage, and my own concern was for this harried writer who had been ambushed by his material, wound up on his hands and knees in a white suit, mopping up a bathroom, and was still facing a ride back in my jeep. If I were permitted one follow-up question, I would ask whether his dry cleaner was able to expunge the interview, or whether the suit had to be replaced.

Addressing the same Design Conference was Brendan Gill, perennial writer and reviewer for the *New Yorker,* chronicler of

Tallulah, and all-purpose gadfly. I felt we had been remiss in not offering lunch to Tom Wolfe and had made sandwiches and a salad. Craggy and urbane, Gill immediately commented on the house's minor architectural features. What, he wanted to know, was the provenance of all these Wrightian touches? I told him that the house had been built in 1947 by Aspen architect Fritz Benedict after five years of study with Frank Lloyd Wright and that it represented a style known locally as Early Fritz. Gill insisted on a tour and almost led me through the three rooms, spinning phrases about recessed lighting and mitred windows. He ducked into the bathroom and stood rapt in front of the window to the carport, one so underappreciated by myself that I seldom remembered to wash it, and pronounced, "The clerestory window off the porte-cochère diffuses a cathedral effulgence that makes this truly the most beautifully illuminated bathroom in North America." At least he didn't notice the dampness underfoot.

Gill ate without comment and attacked the interview with more relish, luxuriating in oratory about the limits of literary criticism. When I asked if he'd like another sandwich, he replied, "That's the first question I haven't been able to answer since 1951." He made some concluding remarks about aging writers, rose to leave, blurted, "But I have to admire this bathroom one more time," and dove through the door. My ears were on point as I sifted the flush. After the briefest of delays Gill emerged unfazed, expressed his gratitude for a most stimulating midday, and was off. There was a fresh tide on the floor, and I would have thought it a reaction to his previous remark if the john hadn't behaved as dismally toward Tom Wolfe. Bad plumbing was turning into a curious test of character: perhaps I should assure myself no more celebrities were due before rousing the plumber.

The john was back in order by the time Harold Clurman arrived for an interview two summers later. Nearing the end of a long career of theater criticism and the first-run direction of many of America's major plays, Clurman was in charge of the first Aspen Playwrights Conference. The interview, scheduled for an August morning, coincided with a cold snap and a visit from my mother. Just before Clurman appeared, I pushed back the splintering bamboo curtains my mother had drawn against the glare, and a sliver of bamboo shot under my nail. Wasn't this the way the Japanese tortured secrets out of GIs during World War II? No amount of maneuvering could pry it loose; I could only hope to fake some hospitality before I got to a doctor.

The editors arrived with a small austere man bundled in a gaberdine overcoat, a wounded look deeping his heavy features. His first comment was to remark how cold the house was. I spun the thermostat and settled Clurman in the armchair from which his predecessors had held forth. My mother offered him a sweet roll, which he accepted and began to devour. She served him coffee and asked if he'd like sugar and cream. "I would have liked sugar," he replied, "but I'm only allowed so much sugar a day. I would much have preferred sugar in my coffee to the sweet roll, but I didn't know about the coffee in time, and now it's too late." Was this man actually going to submit to our questions? If not, could I fly to a doctor?

As soon as the interview began, it was clear that getting Clurman to speak would not be a problem. With each question the answers got louder and more extended until the blood rushed to his face, he gasped for air, and exposed veins could be seen beating on his forehead. Should there be more American theater, at the risk of its being bad? "Yes! I'm all for action. All over . . . theaters in shopping centers and subways, in closets, anywhere. . . . " His hands alternately swung in the air and clenched the arms of the chair, as if they led independent lives. "Bad plays, more bad plays, an enormous *flood* of bad plays, because when you have so many bad plays you are going to have some good ones!" Was this 76-year-old man going to explode in front of us? I had a vision of him expired on my own carpet. We editors had done it with our freezing rooms, our sweet rolls, our perilous questions.

His fervor climaxed when Aspen playwright Hancel McCord asked, "What do you think of Robert Brustein's recent article in the *New York Times,* which declared that the new playwright must move from a Newtonian world to an Einsteinian one, away from the fixed, manipulative world of Arthur Miller?"

"It sounds like shit!" yelled Clurman, then clapped his hand to his mouth and cast a terrified look at my mother. While the word is not among her favorites, she managed a laugh, the gulf was bridged, and we sped the interview to a close. So alarming was Clurman's passion that I even forgot, moments running, my own trial by bamboo.

When Clurman did die of cancer two years later, it was with a chill of assent that I read a eulogy in *The New Republic* by Robert Brustein, the very critic who had provoked Clurman's expletive. Listening to Clurman in a living room was, said Brustein, "like being trapped in a wind tunnel . . . it was impossible not to worry about his health whenever he started talking. Surely no human arteries could endure such exertions, no human heart could take such strains. To see Clurman survive his own lectures was to believe in the indestructibility of the natural tissue, the invincibility of the mortal flesh. When I heard that he had died, I assumed that he had pushed his energy too far, and that Death had clapped him on the shoulder in the middle of a speech." How unnerved Brustein might have been on that cold August morning, when it looked like his own theory was about to send Clurman over the edge.

The only guest who managed to unsettle me before arrival was Joyce Carol Oates. We were offering Oates and her husband a week in Aspen, with a welcoming dinner at my house, in return for a lecture by Oates. It was a mistake to have prepared by reading her fiction, so full of the most uncanny and convincing violence, so knowingly detailed. I had been informed that she did not drink, and had laid in a supply of every imaginable juice and cola. Oates emerged through the carport almost physically projecting quietness with her slender form, her improbable swanlike neck, the pale oval face on which floated the small mouth and enormous nocturnal eyes. I intercepted her in the yard, and asked if I could get her something to drink. She gazed at me with the air of a stunned gazelle. "There's Coke, 7-Up, Pepsi ... Squirt, Dr. Pepper ... orange juice, grape juice..."

"My," she breathed, "so many choices. . ."

Whatever drink she wound up with, her decision-making partook of the timeless. Of the evening, I remember that her husband, English professor Raymond Smith, shy at first, became witty and affable as soon as conversation was underway, and that even Oates made a few comments — about psychometry, about Nixon. But I picture her floating disconnected through the party, a neglected glass in her hand, while even the house as if chastened did not pull any tricks with the curtains or the plumbing, lest it wake her up.

It was only as she left that she burned through the haze by fixing me in the eye and drawling, "You know, if I had a house like this I could *really* write."

I was stunned. For the sake of literature, should I *give* her the place? On the other hand, would the house tire of playing nice and sabotage her career? We are spared the answer, and my conscience was eased the next day when I ran into her on the street, attempted a greeting, and received a reply in a perfect monotone. Here, it appeared, was a kind of somnambulist, simultaneously alien and at home wherever she went. I watched her from a distance with her hair tumbled over her graceful neck, a frumpy overlong dress and a seeming absence in her eyes, as if she were the dumbest tourist of the summer, and realized she had perfected one of the writer's keenest weapons: a perfect anonymity.

Writers claim our attention only by what they accomplish on the page, and their personal eccentricities are material only for trivia like the foregoing. Still, there are those of us for whom well-chosen words are the finest deeds, and those heroes who use them well become objects of study. Writers passing through Aspen no longer need fear our interviews, now that we have withdrawn the life-support system from *Aspen Anthology,* but they may still be attacked by free drinks if they stray into the Jerome Bar. Whatever their personas, they have won our admiration and must suffer the consequences.

16.

Upright Behavior

An amateur pianist without a piano is one of the major social pests of the last century and a half, and as such I stretched the hospitality of several piano-owning Aspenites in the early Sixties. It paid social dividends, sometimes over cocktails, and threw up unusual obstacles, most memorably a rug cleaner who turned hysterical whenever a piano was struck within his earshot, and who ordered his employer to banish me whenever he was on the premises. Instructive, perhaps, but I leapt into my car when someone called from the Aspen Institute to say that a group of upright pianos from the Music School had just gone on sale.

In our culture the piano is still a romantic object, numinous, layered with associations. Its bulk, its meticulous teeth, its polished box that will break into song under hands that can shift its secret panels, all suggest that the piano possesses a hidden spirit, a genie unique to its mysterious case. Within it all keyboard literature lies coiled as an infinity of dreams lies in the sleeper. To select a piano requires the leisure to seek out the genie in the resonance of the bass, the resistance of the keys, the carry of the treble, the gleam of wood, the collaboration with one's own touch, an intuitive sum, not unlike chemistry between persons, that tells you this one, not that one.

I walked into the maintenance building where seven aged uprights loomed from the dark, and a handful of potential buyers were striking chords at random. The finest and most expensive piano had already gone for $40. The two $35 pianos were left, with others for as low as $25. This was no time to coax out genies. I banged a couple of chords on the $35 numbers, put my hand on the one that boomed stoutly back, and said, "I'll take this one."

I was relieved that delivery was included in the purchase price, and had my landlady guide it to the only corner where it wouldn't go through the floor of my two-room rental. It looked splendid next to the shredded couch, but what had I gotten for my $35? I was quite nonplussed at the fullness of sound, particularly in the bass, its autumnal slur, its effortless action; from a mechanical standpoint it was easier to play than the Steinways in other people's living rooms, and would pleasantly corrupt my touch. Over its face curled garlands of floral scrollwork that sprang from a kind of floating urn, and Gothic script above the keyboard proclaimed in gold, *Bush & Gerts, Chicago.* I looked inside. A decal on the lid guaranteed the piano against defective workmanship or material for ten years. A metal bar across the action bore three entwined circles framing, in succession, Columbus taking his first portentous step onto the New World, the legend, "World's Columbian Exposition, in memory of the four hundredth anniversary of the landing of Columbus, 1492-1892," and a Maltese cross logo that proclaimed, *The Bush & Gerts Reliable.* These quirky uprights, I learned, had been unloaded because they required too much tuning, and were being replaced by an armada of shrill, metallic, nasal little spinets that shared the same tin soul. The Music School was no doubt relieved.

But the restless probably shouldn't have pianos any more than they should have pets. Not long after I installed the piano in its corner, I decided to go to Europe for a few months. I stored books and sheet music in a basement in Denver where they perished in a flood, left favorite clothing with an Aspen laundry that lost it, and lent the piano to a friend with the request that he keep tabs on it if he couldn't keep it, and not let it escape the valley. As it happened I was away for three years — because of another Chicago upright. I wandered into an Andalusian night club where the local band was braying next to a familiar unplayed object. That became the first of a three-year succession of night club jobs that made America — and particularly my possessions there — seem remote and theoretical. But when I found my way back to Aspen and settled into the annex of the Floradora, the possession I most craved was the Bush & Gerts. Not every lodge will let you room with your piano, but the Floradora was one of Aspen's looser ships, and those were days before the separate music campus, when students poured a sweet cacophony from rooms all over town. Experimental pianist William Masselos, in any case, would drown me out from his apartment in back. The Bush & Gerts had changed hands several times in my absence, and had passed to a black lady who loved it. I had no idea what its previous custodian had told her and felt bad about reclaiming it, but the piano was delivered uncomplainingly to my room.

After several months in the Floradora I bought the home I have lived in ever since. The house itself was furnished, my own possessions were thinned, and the move's single challenge was to transport the piano the few blocks down Main Street. The Floradora had by then developed a rude subculture, and I had elicited a late-afternoon pledge from the most able-bodied to help with the move. I had laid in a case of beer at the other end, and planned to turn the occasion into a surprise party and preliminary housewarming. I knocked at Dave's door. "I'm in the shower," he screamed. "I can't move a piano *wet*." From Konstantine's room came no sound even of breath: he was in samadhi, or out. And so it went with my committed crew. The owner of a pickup, another dupe and myself wound up loading one of the densest, meanest, most treacherous objects ever foaled by man, and I learned that the genie of an upright being disturbed converts to that of a mule. The struggle sapped even the taste for beer, for a party never ignited and a second lesson was learned: never brandish the stick without also dangling the carrot.

The Bush & Gerts endured several years of my daily two-hour pounding — then the Music School offered another deal: new Japanese grands were being sold at the end of the season for 20% off, after serving two months in a practice room. Priced higher than the upright by a factor of a hundred, it was still a deal, and time to trade up. Unbelievably, the selection process was no more ceremonious than the previous one. The grands were still in practice rooms in use by students who had signed up for precious hours, and who were outraged to be interrupted by anything so low as a salesman with a client. I could feel them glaring at me from the heights of their technique as I ventured a few chords and runs on the options, then picked. The salesman then discovered bits of tape on the strings of my selection, revealing that it had been used for an experimental piece that involved attaching nuts and bolts, and leading me to wonder whether I'd mischosen. The stalled virtuoso wasn't about to put up with an investigation, and we left hoping for the best. Ten days later the piano was delivered to my house, to my shock, by a single man, who wheeled it out of a truck, screwed on the legs and righted it with an ease that seems, looking back, pure levitation. "With levers and a dolly," he said, "it's a cinch."

"It took three of us to get the upright in here," I said.

"Only three for an *upright*? You must have been geniuses."

If the Kawai and the Bush & Gerts were in any way matched for sound, or even in the same room, it would have been tempting to keep them for duo piano, but I really had my eye on the upright's spot for a bookshelf and a rocker. Yet some weakness about the romance of pianos would not let me offer it for sale, or relinquish possession. As if it were a prize hound I wanted to be able to seize it back in case of neglect or abuse. I would lend it to anyone who promised to take

care of it, and who would do the moving. It went first to a composition student who moved into town for a couple of years and married locally. When she left, it filtered through several more houses, and wound up with friends who moved it into their son's bedroom in hopes that he had musical talent, and where it functioned as an unwanted room divider. The Kawai, meanwhile, survived a succession of renters as handily as it survived the nuts and bolts — for I had begun spending winters at my mother's house outside Phoenix.

One morning in Phoenix a friend told me over breakfast that he was interested in learning the piano, had hoped to inherit his mother's, but learned some acquisitive cousins had gotten first dibs. "If you come to Aspen," I heard myself say, "I will give you a piano." I gave him a short history of the Bush & Gerts, and told him all he would have to do was to haul it to Phoenix. While I have occasionally given presents that cost over $35, I have never given anything so exalted as a piano, and felt a delicious flush.

My friend and another Phoenician showed up the following Fourth of July, and after an exhausting weekend our last duty was to see the piano into the U-Haul. It was still lodged in the room of the unpianistic son, and the house was unoccupied. Again there were three of us, and the piano was on its worst behavior. Trying not to gash the dresser, ball up the rug, gouge the walls and unhinge the front door, we pulled, eased, jimmied, yanked, butted, cursed, and started over. "I hope the piano isn't more trouble than it's worth," I gasped.

"It's the thought that counts," my friend gasped back.

I felt a chill: with some gifts it's the thought that counts, but with a piano it's the *piano* that counts.

My friend phoned from Phoenix two days later to report that it had been a wild trip back: they were accelerating toward Monday jobs when they discovered there were no all-night gas stations in southeast Utah. At 3 A.M. they tried to rouse a lodge owner — a person who was, in fact, my single acquaintance on that stretch. When he didn't answer their ring, they resorted to self-serve and started siphoning from his truck, intending to pin a few bills under his wiper. Without warning he appeared in his pajamas, looking in the dark like a B-movie psychopath. They leapt to the car and gunned it with the piano swinging mulishly in their wake, having rustled enough gas to make it to the all-night stations in Kayenta. But the piano had reached his living room unscathed.

I looked forward to seeing how far my friend had progressed the following winter. Well, he said on my arrival, he hadn't really gotten started yet. And so it went, year after year, as the piano stood in his living room. Worse still, instead of music a book I had written was positioned on the music rack, and on the lid perched a stuffed iguana I had once given him. If this was what it felt like to be a cult figure, frankly I preferred music, and surely the piano's genie did too. I knew that the move from thin mountain air to urbanized desert would do the action no good, but the piano was also losing ivory keys that couldn't be replaced. We are, gratefully, no longer turning elephants into pianos, but it seemed to me we ought to protect those keyboards still laid out in tusk. This was mere piano neglect, not abuse, and the friendship outweighed even the piano. But how to salvage both? To make matters worse, a piano tuner told me that at the end of the last century there were 1,500 to 2,000 piano companies in the United States, some of which built only a few dozen specimens. Pianos were built in kitchens and backyards, often by German cabinetmakers; they were the TVs of their day. "Mr. Bush and Mr. Gerts worked independently for most of their lives, and only collaborated for a few years. The Bush & Gerts is more or less the Rolls Royce of uprights." I repeated this lore to my friend, who looked uncomfortable. Suddenly he was facing a move, and asked if he could store the piano with a friend. I was quick to offer to store it myself, sure he would never want it back.

He arrived with the piano in a pickup driven by the friend who had accompanied him to Aspen. This time the piano slid effortlessly from the truck to a room off my mother's carport, as if it were headed back to the barn. Some Chicagoans, I thought, will do anything to retire to the Southwest. "Thanks for letting me borrow the piano," said my friend. "I really appreciate it."

I nearly blurted, "But it wasn't a loan, it was a gift!" Sense caught my tongue. Whether this was a misconception or a face-saving inspiration, it was the perfect solution — for the friendship and for the piano — and all I had to do was shut up. Again I had laid in some beers, and we downed them all.

But the family grand also resides at my mother's and there is little motivation, even for me, to play the Bush & Gerts. It should be restored. It should be given to a deserving prodigy. It idles, glaring at me like a musical albatross. But there is a finite supply of throaty vintage uprights, some cracking in Michigan garages, some being atomized by Bolivian insects. The survivors are still charged with the world's music, ready to croon in voices that may be bettered, but never duplicated. Their inhabiting genies are hanging tough, and at this rate I will probably be throwing a centennial birthday bash for mine in 1992.

17.

Joy's Treadmill

The requirements of the exercise trail are far stricter than those of the path that leads through mere scenery. It must be steep and of a steady pitch. It should be close to home, so one doesn't waste time commuting. And since one is there to build muscle, lose weight, and tone up the system, the setting should be pleasant but monotonous enough not to distract those who, in the spirit of self-conquest, are not climbing a mountain so much as they are scaling themselves. It should, in short, resemble as closely as possible the Ute Trail, that nineteen-switchback self-punishment that takes off from Ute Avenue, on Aspen's east end, and emerges on a rocky perch a thousand feet above town.

Not that the Ute Trail insults the eye. It begins almost invisibly as a slender rut between small aspens, scrub oak, Rocky Mountain maples, and low vegetation, then climbs, darkening, through spruce and Douglas fir, gradually modulating from open meadow to deep forest. Views in glimpses through trees broaden and deepen until one breaks, dramatically, into the open on the top rock. Some twenty-five miles of the Roaring Fork Valley lie spread below, from Independence Pass to Snowmass Canyon, and the village braying at your feet, familiar from aerial postcards, is Aspen. Newcomers will spend considerable time remarking that the Opera House looks like the hotel on the Monopoly board, that the construction sites look grander than anything yet built, and that it is impossible to compose it all in a viewfinder. The trail's habitués tend to pause only long enough to glance at a stopwatch, or stop short of the rock itself and leave the rigors of appreciation to first-timers and tourists.

Exercise buffs, in fact, hike quite a different trail from the novice who takes in his surroundings. Typically they arrive in sweatsuits or jogging shorts, often with ears clamped in a Walkman that severs any connection between audio and visual stimuli. Instead of scenery, they perceive a private mythology composed of such totems as Pole Turn, the Bear's Den (no bears), the Traverse, the Dip, Window Turn, the Handle, the Corkscrew, Root 66, Choreography Turn, Stopwatch Rock. Nor are regulars in pairs and groups any more engrossed in the scenery. Here, for instance, are a few conversational scraps I picked up over the course of a season:

"How much did he lose on his garage in Rifle?"

"By then you'll be so drunk you won't even realize ..."

"... dozens of tiny Japanese warplanes ..."

"It's not what *I'd* call stereophonic."

"My father will spend all day cooking chili, ribs, all kinds of foods that aren't typical to Israel."

More attuned to his situation was the stranger in the peaked cap, on his way down as I hiked up, who stepped off the trail, held out his palm to the five kids trailing him, and said, "Y'all prepare to *yield*."

How did Aspen acquire this gym? The Bureau of Land Management, previous owner of the land, had developed a program whereby a municipality could annex contiguous BLM land if they made it useful to citizens. In 1967 the city applied for 81.53 acres and paid a man $7,000 to build any kind of trail he chose to the scenic rock. He surveyed it on horseback, then cut it steep and fast. The land transfer was approved two years later, allowing the city to possess the slope for twenty-five years for the grand sum of $20.38 a year. Ute Trail, so perfect for exercise and so calamitous for the casual stroll, is thus the means by which the city captured some spectacular real estate as quickly and cheaply as possible.

The exercise is perfect, at least, on the uphill, where a swift regular claims to average seventeen minutes for an ascent and estimates that a swifter high schooler might shave that by three minutes. The downhill is also prized by some for toning up the tops of thighs for skiing. It is true that when the trail is moist one can dance to the bottom like Nureyev the Coyote, but as soon as the surface dries, mysterious cinders detach themselves from underfoot and pepper the slope with pulverized ball bearings, launching the unwary hiker feet-forward into the arms of ascending strangers and gashing the heels of his palms as he tries to catch himself. Extending the season into late fall, I once inched up a still worse surface composed of snow that had melted and congealed, then picked my way down pitched ice as the early dusk turned to night, taking an hour and a half for a descent the same swift regular accomplishes in nine minutes.

Joggers may have missed it, but there is plenty of seasonal change for those deploying their eyes. During summer months the lower slopes vibrate with cycles of penstemon, wild rose, paintbrush, columbine, wild geranium, salsify, mariposa lilies, wild asters, and fireweed. I have seen both deer and blue grouse on the trail itself, and while the area is less than prime birding, I am a poor enough athlete to have spotted flickers, jays, Oregon juncos, nuthatches, solitary thrushes, pine siskins, and Townsend's solitaires. And once, pausing for breath, I heard and felt a rush of air against the back of my neck that was either a falcon or a mystic experience.

Even the upper switchbacks, with their vertical trees, horizontal branches, and slopes falling away at some fifty degrees, have become more various since the freak snowstorm of June, 1984. Pine trees have evolved to hold carloads of snow without tipping over, but they do so best when the frozen ground locks their roots into place. On this occasion an unusually thick snowmelt had turned the steep slopes to mush, and century-old firs bent under fresh wet snow and toppled, torn out by the roots. Trees on the downhill side, with their roots under the trail, uprooted parts of the trail itself, leaving pits walled by root systems that resemble clotted cartwheels. Trunks tumbled in parallel give slopes an appearance of water blurred as it rushes downstream. The treefall reaches its climax on the last traverse, which passes between chainsawed trunks as timber caught midair rockets sideways and arcs over the trail in tangles of oblique lines. "Crashed majors of a final panorama," said the poet Richard Wilbur, of other matters, but something about these downed trees evokes that impressive line.

The Friday after the great blizzard, physicist and Ute Trail regular Jeremy Bernstein headed up the switchbacks and found that fallen trees had made them impassable. To be turned back was intolerable to someone who had taken the trail every second summer day "since the Utes finished it," climbed in his own private mythology from the tropical to the arctic ecosystems, and practiced a variant ascent that involved taking the trail "the canonical way," then scaling the top rock by means of a lateral chimney. He returned on Monday to size up the problem before recruiting volunteers, to find that unknown Samaritans over the weekend had put the trail immediately back in service. The Samaritans, it turned out, were Dave Wise and an assistant, in charge of trail maintenance for the county, who labored two days with chain saws and shovels, knowing, perhaps, that if they delayed they would be facing fanatics like Jeremy on withdrawal symptoms.

For the Ute Trail is one more Aspen addiction. Like a dog that looks at you moistly and then begins to revolve in front of your footstool, at the accustomed hour the body begins to rev even as the brain says, shut up and let me *read*. The body always wins, and soon even the mind is content to be ticking off the Traverse, Window Turn, the Corkscrew, back on joy's treadmill.

18.

Is Aspen Real?

A friend from Phoenix recently banged on my door, clutching a map of Aspen. She'd wasted most of the morning trying to find Hallam Lake with it — would I kindly explain, using this map, how to get there. I spread it on the table. Aside from cartoon versions of prominent buildings popping up here and there, it seemed a standard plat of town. "Here's your lodge," I said, drawing with my finger, "and here's Hallam Lake. You just go down Mill to Puppy Smith Street."

"But what *direction* is that?"

"Away from the ski mountain."

"But the mountain is south of town, and north is at the top of all maps. The ski mountain is at the top of this map. And there are no little arrows to tell you what direction is what."

"The ski mountain is at the top of all maps of Aspen. Everyone sees the town facing the Mountain."

"I did try to pick up some clues," she persisted. "For instance, here's West End Avenue."

"West End Avenue is at the extreme east end of town," I said, folding the map. "I'll give you a lift to Hallam Lake."

This tense little exchange led to thoughts about our innocent grid in the mountains. Except where watercourses interfere, Aspen is simplicity squared — every corner a right angle, every block as quadrangular as the American flag. Yet somehow it has never made sense to me either. I started off wrong when I first visited here, arriving in Glenwood Springs by train. I would get picked up and driven south — I thought — to Aspen. I entered town over that north-south span, Castle Creek Bridge. I know now, conceptually, that Highway 82 curves eastward from Glenwood, imperceptibly rotating the cardinal points ninety degrees by the time it gets here. Decades later I still can't fathom it. I look south from my window, up Castle Creek toward Albuquerque, and feel myself looking west toward Los Angeles.

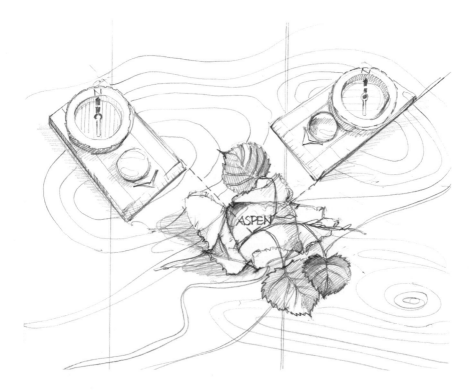

The longer one lives in Aspen, the less important it seems to get a grip on the fundamentals. It is axiomatic that the only ones who can name the streets are those who deplaned last week, and that locals only remember streets that have restaurants named for them. Recently a veteran of twenty summer music festivals, trying to explain the location of this summer's house, made several false starts, then said in perfect Aspenese, "It's on the corner closest to the Jerome and farthest from the Mountain." And who but a postman could distinguish between Hopkins, Hyman and Hallam?

Granted that when the baffled call Aspen "unreal," more than bad geography is implied. Some of it stems from such touches as being asked to remove your shoes to attend a garage sale run on Japanese principles. Or playing warm-up catch at a performance workshop and being instructed to watch the tennis ball's aura. Or the gas man borrowing, and not returning, your copy of *African Genesis.* Former State Highway Commissioner Dick Prosence announced at a hearing in 1969 that the purpose of four-laning Highway 82 was to connect Aspen with the United States. Maintaining that attitude is a page in the *Aspen Daily News* called "The Real World," featuring news clips about events happening anywhere but here.

Philosophically it is fatuous to claim that Aspen isn't real; an item need occur only once to earn that distinction. Aspen is only improbable. Digging deep, I suspect one would discover that Aspen's sense of unreality ultimately springs from the kind of guilt feeling that equates reality with misery. To the extent that Aspen is under-represented by starvation, crime, urban blight, unemployment, racial intolerance and the like, Aspen is unreal, and Aspenites maintain their sophistication by admitting it. Aspen may be over-represented by transience, high cost of living, substance abuse, insularity, and wood smoke, but its flaws aren't gritty enough to consider mainstream. While most of the world struggles to survive, Aspenites go to the mat over matters of décor. The town may simply be nervous about taking itself seriously when its leading product is fun.

So Aspen's sense of dislocation doubtless involves more than the fact that most Aspenites would probably scan the wrong quadrant of the sky for the North Star. But these mountains have begun the process by walling us in. By air they give us as much orientation as the crosscurrents of an ocean, and we step onto tarmac literally at sea. We reach Aspen by car from Glenwood Springs with south gradually mutating into east, or over Independence Pass — the half-year that it is open — trending west-northwest by means of every direction there is. By whatever mode, one arrives at a place that is geographically, if not culturally, cut loose, and if the mapmaker knows the compass points, he isn't telling. Geology, to a degree, is destiny, and if Aspenites feel out of touch with the real world, perhaps they aren't quite sure in which direction it lies.

19.

Rolling the Odds

It used to be my conception of hell to be haunted by the eyes of all the hitchhikers I was afraid to pick up. Of course that was before *est* destroyed my conscience. It was also before a certain episode that took place between Carbondale and Glenwood Springs.

My earliest encounters with hitchhiking, as a rider, were innocent enough. Having the run of Hermes, my father's Mercury, and being terrified of strangers, from the age of sixteen I simply drove myself where I wanted to go, alone. But at college Hermes broke down, and my roommate talked me into hitching rather than cancel a weekend in New York. Over an hour we suffered a cold wind on the Merritt Parkway, then a primeval Ford with a black man at the wheel pulled over and let us in. I braced for my last ride, but by the time we reached Manhattan the driver and I had succeeded in recollecting all the themes of the Chopin nocturnes, in order. My defenses were further lowered in Spain, where my Citröen was confiscated for being improperly licensed and I traveled frequently *por autostop* — but Andalusians seem less menacing to life and limb than fellow Americans.

It wasn't until the late Sixties, back in the States, when youthful solidarity was at its zenith, Kerouac had become patron saint of The Road, and love was a painful duty, that it became imperative to offer one's compatriots, however unappealing, a lift. Generosity was no longer moral, it was political: and among the non sequiturs that blossomed out of the war, to share one's wheels was one more way to show up the pigs, to roll in the new freedom and keep faith with the future.

And solidarity was rewarding. I spent an hour with a University of Wisconsin graduate who told me he had leaked news to the student paper that the university was working on a secret contract with the Department of Defense, which led in turn to the bombing of the physics laboratory by persons he didn't know, and an FBI tail on him ever since. I picked up a bewildered young man who had just returned from Vietnam to Newcastle, to find his family had left with

103

no forwarding address. There were endless locals, with or without dogs, cigarettes, skis and other impedimenta, with whom one discussed snow conditions, potholes and other topics that left no trace. And rides in silence, steeped in humanitarianism.

Surviving it neatly, I branched out. Near Kayenta I picked up a young Anglo who was teaching school with the Navajos and could, I felt, have become a friend for life. In Tuba City I stopped for a weathered old man with a white cloth around his forehead and a white kerchief slung from his neck, both bloody. I asked him where he was headed. "Henh!" he declared in a sharp nasal. I rephrased the question and got the same reply; it was clear he spoke no English. Several miles down the road we approached three young Navajos hitching. The old man issued a stern command in Navajo. The back of my Jeep was full of camping equipment and I had no intention of stopping. The old man commanded again and grabbed my arm. Fearing he didn't understand the danger of automobiles, I stopped and the young Navajos piled in. For the first time I felt that the car was out of my control. I turned south toward Flagstaff while the Navajos chatted among themselves. I asked one of the young ones where the old man was going.

"Hanks. It's still a way ahead."

"What's happened to him?"

The young man shrugged. Soon we arrived at Hanks Trading Post, where the young men bailed out and thanked me, and the old man snorted and slapped the air angrily in my direction.

Fear and curiosity in me are delicately and perhaps dangerously balanced, and I continued to pick up or ignore strangers, according to mood, until the morning I was on my way to soak a hangover in the Glenwood pool. At the turnoff to Carbondale I stopped for a tall blond person of indeterminate gender, bearing some sort of parcel. Installed in the passenger seat, the person materialized a kind of lanky bonelessness, a seven-day beard and eyes like bleached denim, while the package appeared to be a plastic dry cleaning bag full of spray cans. He kept floundering with the ends of the bag to keep the cans from falling out. When I eased off at 60 miles an hour, he leaned into me, extended a hand, and said, "Muh name's Chuck."

"Glad to meet you, Chuck," I said, with a nod toward a hand I was in no position to shake.

He sprawled back to his side and a spray can fell out of the plastic and toward the door. Apparently thinking it would pass on through, he simultaneously made a grab for it and opened the door, catching it slightly outside the car, while in a flash I envisioned him splashed on the pavement and myself charged with manslaughter.

When the errant can was back in the plastic and my adrenaline leveled off, I asked what was in the cans. He made no reply. Presently he reached for a rag out of his back pocket. This is it, I thought, I'm about to be chloroformed. He removed a can, sprayed gold paint into the rag, held it to his nose and breathed deeply. His body slumped further.

"Jes come from Chicago," he said. "Bad place. Nobody there'll help you much. On my way to Utah, little town I grew up in. My brother's there, they're keeping him in an insane asylum. Hell, he ain't insane. I'm gonna get him out." We sped in silence while I digested that information. Then he added, "Hey, can you give me some money?"

At 60 miles an hour I thought the 12 miles would never end. I pulled up exhausted to City Market in Glenwood Springs, let him out and handed him two quarters. The money, partly the last insult, was also sheer thanksgiving for surviving my latest good deed before I repaired to the Glenwood pool for a long, contemplative soak.

Since then my inner balance is less delicate, more firmly tipped away from curiosity, toward fear. I am aware that Aspen violin cases do not usually contain machine guns, and prefer to give a local a lift. But the eyes of hell have transformed for me from a jury of rejected strangers into a single known pair: of bleached denim.

20.

The Face Is Familiar

Aspenites who spend parts of their lives elsewhere know well the burdens of representing Aspen, the national crisis. When the Claudine scandal caught me in Phoenix, for instance, I got a call from a Scottsdale barber shop asking for the inside story. I reported, truthfully, that I had never heard of Spider or Claudine, but I thought Andy Williams was a singer — the kind of ignorance that has allowed me a certain distance from our popular serial. This very reluctance to play ambassador may have provoked a local curse, because for reasons that have nothing to do with living here I seem to remind people of the most famous Aspenite of them all. Months can go by with no reference being made, then it will strike three times in one week. Often I can see it coming in the play of hesitation and risk that crosses a stranger's face just before the dread phrase is pronounced: "You look like John Denver."

I have studied the possibility in the mirror. We wear glasses from the same shop, and our dullish blond hair hangs mid-ear. There, to *my* eyes, the impersonation ends. Yet from dark bars to dental clinics, under gas tubing and by daylight, the allegation keeps tripping me up. At the beginning of an expedition to some remote Baja caves, for example, a woman told me she kept expecting me to burst into song.

"Do I look that eager to get on a mule?" I asked.

'No, you look like J--n D----r."

A man next to me in a Phoenix bar turned and said, "You know, you keep reminding me of someone, and I can't think who it is."

"Michael York?" I offered.

"No ..." he said, as if actually considering it, and I left him considering as I sped to a far stool.

One of the advantages of being in the real Aspen, I have thought, is that at least here people know what our lead tenor looks like. Yet I have fished for a seat at the movies while a voice from the darkness breathed, "That's him!" And finally a local bartender spoke the fateful words. When I expressed surprise, he said that he had been Denver's road manager, and should know.

Why would anyone resent resembling his town's most popular monument? I am, in fact, enthusiastic about John Denver the benefactor, who uses his position to attack world hunger and environmental pillage, whose benefits keep local institutions afloat, and who has launched a problem-solving foundation — particularly when other stars are blowing their fortunes and their brains. But I am being likened, I'm afraid, to John Denver the entertainer, of the ambrosial voice, the hygienic repertoire, the carmelized TV shows, who hymns our crowded valley to the saturation point, and whose sedative warbling pursues me into far corners where strangers are already eyeing me appraisingly. Besides, I had this face before he did; people should properly be comparing him to me. By now I should be resigned to it, but when I hear myself compared to John Denver, I feel like leaving on a jet plane.

How, then, to respond? Most sensibly by feigning surprise and changing the subject. But coincidence itself impresses me, and the implausibility of resembling someone from my own small town usually pries it forth. In an expansive mood — and ignoring the various distances between Main Street and Starwood — I remark that we are, in fact, practically neighbors. Less charmed, I may report, as was once the case, that the last time I saw John Denver was when he jaywalked in front of my car on the way to City Hall, and only good brakes saved the facial plagiarist.

Yet I am nearly missing a good bet, for several years ago a friend of mine, of Denver's general build and hair style, made serious money as a stand-in. I have since cased the potential myself. It was in City Market, just after a dislocating nap, and I found myself saying hello to a familiar customer whose name I had blanked. Two aisles later I realized it was akin to forgetting my own name — for the figure back at cheese was That Singer, whom I had never actually met. When we were stalled in the express line together I compared frames. He turned out to be slightly taller and narrower than I, and no doubt has become narrower since. There may be good money in resembling John Denver from the back, but none that I know of from the neck up.

Never, until this therapeutic confession, have I volunteered this likeness I am still blind to — with one exception. One Christmas my mother was watching a John Denver special in Phoenix and asked if I'd like to join her in the living room for some shots of Aspen. I paused before breaking it to someone whose genes I had inherited, then I said, "Some people have said that I look like John Denver."

"You do not look like that jack-o-lantern," she shot back. "Although, you do remind me a bit of Dick Cavett."

I have been assured that in the future I will not look like John Denver, because he is moving to contact lenses and longer (in some versions, shorter) hair. I hope the public snaps up the new image. Meanwhile, an incident that took place recently in Holbrook, Arizona, has made me slightly less touchy on the subject. It was painfully early on a Monday in June. I was having breakfast at the window table of a café and recovering from a beerfest for which my departure from Phoenix had provided the excuse. A Native American, thirtyish, unsteady of foot and looking as if he were recovering from a more perilous weekend than mine, stopped dead in his tracks. He grinned through the window, then reeled into the café trailed by two companions. The sidekicks wanted to sit on the far side, but the one who had stared insisted on their taking the table next to mine. Once the friends were seated he continued to my chair, smiled with utter radiance, and said, "You look li' Joh' Debber." His friends commanded him to sit down and behave, and a waitress shot across the room and told him to stop hassling the customers. For the first time, I felt warmed by the illusion, and for the first time the moment was cut off. We smiled helplessly and shrugged, condemned to our separate recoveries. I hope that the world's image of John Denver will change as he changes himself. I also hope, in some remote corner of myself, that Holbrook will remember him as he was.

21.

Sunday in the Tent With Jorge

It is the belief of John Cage, inventor of the musical happening, that music is the perception of notes plus everything else going on at the same time. A rendition of Schubert, for instance, may consist of four movements, the man to your right fiddling with his program, a shaft of cologne from behind, great waves of sneezing and coughing, a matron in front snapping awake, four fiddlers bobbing like weeds in the wind, an itch on your shoulder blade, and all the unregistered scuffling, wheezing, squirming and indecipherable shivers of air. And in Aspen this phantasmagoria has been surrounded by a succession of tents.

The first of these tents was designed in 1949 by Finnish architect Eero Saarinen, an airy and graceful canvas slung over free-standing wooden poles that swung wildly in midsummer winds and gave one daymares of being crushed. Cows still wandered through the surrounding meadow, punctuating the occasional arpeggio with a questioning moo. Buffeted by wind, rain, and freak snowfalls, the canvas has been replaced twice. In 1964, the tent itself was redesigned by Bauhaus architect Herbert Bayer so that the teetering poles were replaced with a permanent steel skeleton, a cement dish full of benches offered seating for 1600, and the tent attained the poise of a permanent building.

But unlike urban concert halls, the tent invites the natural into the artificial, and glories in the modulations of weather. The main entrance and two side openings keep the air lively, sunlight diffuses into a soft radiance, and the entire tent flaps, swells, almost breathes like a living creature. The shadows of aspens toss a spangled calligraphy onto the sides, magpies streak overhead like birds of pure thought, and the entire conjunction of cloud, sunlight and sound invents a feast of correspondence. I remember a day of grey weather when woodwinds in falling thirds began Ravel's *Introduction and Allegro.* As the solo harp swept in with a brilliant run, the sun burst through and flooded the tent with gold, as if one could see the sound of the harp — or hear the sun.

Some effects are less transcendent. Midsummer concerts seem coordinated with squalls that store up wind, lightning, thunder, and rain for the slow movements. The cows of yesteryear have been replaced by the distant wails, snarls, whines and drones of ambulances, trail bikes, chain saws, and passing planes. Those who sprawl on the grass outside to sip wine, work on their tans and listen gratis, often abuse the privilege with shrieking children and barking dogs. Interference, while not overwhelming, has generated a minor folklore. The ear-splitting torrents that used to greet Valenti's harpsichord have passed to Laszlo Varga, whose cello solos are tantamount to a rain dance. In a change of luck one summer he began Kodály's *Sonata for Cello Alone* under a peerless sky, only to be joined by a siren. Partisans of pure acoustics have never been happy, and in 1964 a plan surfaced to replace the Saarinen tent with a permanent cinderblock enclosure. The notion succumbed, possibly to economics, possibly to a handful of crank letters from persons like myself who believed, with Cage, that Aspen's music is more than fine sound. The merits of sun and fresh air versus downpours and squad cars, however, is not a matter I would care to discuss with Mr. Varga.

So the tent lives, charged with extramusical association. On entering one is handed a program with the week's musical lineup, names of orchestra personnel, biographies of soloists, a brief history of the festival, local ads and an extensive catalog of benefactors, sponsors, patrons, sustaining members, contributing members, and members, lovingly divided according to size of donation so the bored listener can delve into comparative generosity. At the program's heart lie the notes by Kurt Oppens. Often considered the finest annotations at any contemporary season, Oppens's prose ranges beyond music into history and philosophy, reflects his sweeping knowledge of English and German literature, and adds the excursions of thought to the containment of sound.

Events like master classes create categories of their own. Public lessons given by prominent soloists and faculty members to their own and each others' students, the sessions provide a good way to learn the literature in depth, offer free lessons if one plays the piece oneself, and give exposure to young performers sometimes destined for — or already touched with — greatness. Meanwhile one gains insight into the teachers themselves. One, for instance, lectures brilliantly at the beginning of each class on topics as diverse as Mallarmé, Thomas Mann, the Bicentennial, and the state of contemporary music, and one summer used the occasion as a platform to attack a composer-in-residence whose work he disapproved.

Another delivered a full half hour of stories about people falling off piano benches while a student sat on stage in terror of the Rachmaninoff prelude she never got to play. Master classes are vastly underrated as arcane entertainment.

Also unattended is the three-week contemporary series featuring music of the twentieth century, works by composers-in-residence and pieces commissioned by the festival itself. Such well-known composers as Darius Milhaud, Aaron Copland, Eliott Carter, and George Crumb join the unknowns who win Pulitzer prizes in the kinds of events necessary to keep music alive, to prevent it from becoming only a showcase for the past. The slight attendance and difficult listening are a sad reflection on our splintering culture. One can stumble onto some exciting discoveries, but the sounds are often galling and the Philistine's best ploy is to take the concert as a happening in the hope of being seriously offended. Over the years I have seen pianos beaten, climbed on and assaulted from behind, amplified water glasses played with bows, cellos crooning like whales, lullabies for oboe, snare drum and tape deck, sustained farts for brass, violas like nightingales dying of nerve gas, and once a man in a karate suit ran screaming and beat a score of Chinese gongs that lined the tent's circumference. My greatest contemporary thrill was to help pianist William Masselos unprepare a prepared piano. The sacred festival Steinway had been rigged with screws, washers, nuts, and bolts so that it sounded like a Balinese gamelan orchestra, for a piece so seldom played, explained Masselos, that one wrote to John Cage for the score, the original hardware, and a set of instructions.

Over the years the festival has generated a few eccentricities. I am personally a proud member of the Comissiona Fan Club, dedicated to the annual guest appearance of Sergiu Comissiona, Czech-born conductor of the Baltimore Symphony. We wait for his arrival the way small children wait for Santa Claus, haunt orchestra rehearsals, and take our position at concerts close to the side, where by experiment we have found we miss the least of his dance. It is our weird joy to watch Comissiona lean forward and saw with the cellos, pick notes of the piccolo out of midair, puff his cheeks with the horns, advance into the sound like a matador, then step back in marionette ballet and point to a soloist as if to say, "Do it!" With others it may be a passion for pianists or, in current ascendancy, strings: Yo-Yo Ma or Zara Nelsova on cello, Pinchas Zukerman on viola and violin. And with everyone it is Itzhak Perlman, whose fiddling draws like Mick Jagger.

The openest secret is the Sunday morning orchestra rehearsal, when one can hear the popular afternoon program with scarcely a break. Jorge Mester conducts with his dog Rags heaped at his feet. The music is far more resonant without all that flesh and clothing to sop up the sound, and the soloist, being fresher, often gives a freer performance. No fidgeting backs, no ugly heads: in an empty tent one is George III with full orchestra playing for oneself and one's court.

Local participation sometimes evades public knowledge. While newspaper criticism probably means less in Aspen than anywhere else, for many years the *Aspen Times* has sponsored a reviewer. Music critics were formerly recruited from the festival itself, and had to remain anonymous to avoid being felled from behind by a sharpened bow. Since there is nothing like a mystery to spawn detectives, for several summers a cabal of musicians and reporters, not altogether distinct from the Comissiona Fan Club, pored over the list of festival participants to debate and narrow the field. The *Times* office was closely watched for the arrival of unmarked manila envelopes. A crucial suspect was challenged to a round of Facts in Five to obtain a handwriting sample. Once *Times* editor Bil Dunaway was innocently asked why the music review was late; when Bil jumped out the door as if he had forgotten something, the questioner tailed him — unsuccessfully — toward his rendezvous. All reviewers, from The Syndicate to Phil S. Stein, were eventually unmasked. One turned out to be none other than Jon Busch, then a visiting bassoonist, now a local; another was a festival official. And one, realizing he was discovered, refused to write further copy. Stunned with guilt, the detectives realized they had gone too far. . . .

As music lovers converge on the tent for reasons artistic or nefarious, so do musicians infuse the town. Before the Aspen Music School acquired its campus on Castle Creek, most practice took place within Aspen itself. One heard Albert Tipton's flute by the post office, George Gaber's percussion over the foreign car garage, and students squeaking, banging, pealing, tootling, plunking, screeching, bellowing, pounding, and caterwauling from open windows until the town brayed like a Serengeti waterhole, or a symphony by Ives. The clamor has dispersed into practice rooms and far lodges and condominiums, tempering the invasion, but as citizens, many musicians have quietly dug in. Some have invested in apartments, bought or built houses, partly in defense against rents that have skyrocketed to the point where full-time players only break even, or actually lose money, for the mere privilege of summering in Aspen. But for many whose career keeps them on the move, or who transfer from one symphony orchestra to another, Aspen is the single constant in their lives. Changing as the town changes, they throw down roots: to a jetting troubadour even Aspen can seem like home.

It is a tribute to Aspen's presence that even music, that most self-contained of the arts, becomes charged with concentric rings of association. Looking back it is difficult to separate the festival from the smell of canvas, improvisations of light, the bite of the lemonade stand's coffee or Kurt Oppens' thought, gossip at intermission group enthusiasm, and discrete preference — until one would have to agree with John Cage that music is everything that happens while the music lasts, or with John Muir that everything in the universe is hitched to everything else. But the music only lasts nine weeks. While one is careening in an unholy glut between nonstop events, greasing time's passage, the last cadence is speeding to meet one. There is a final ovation, then it happens. Like a burst bubble the musicians scatter to separate careers, visitors go home, the classical big top is folded away, and the locals reach wearily for their records, lest a silence settle around them like snow.

22.

Reinventing the Wheeler

If tragedian James O'Neill returned to the stage of the Wheeler Opera House after an absence of nearly a hundred years, he would feel at ease. The prismatic crystal, the vibrant carpets and walls, the horseshoe sweep of the mezzanine would betray no intervening saga of fire, financial ruin, and redecoration by that austere German school, the Bauhaus. If anything upset his soliloquies, it would be the peculiar audience — an audience largely responsible for returning the Wheeler to its reassuring splendor.

By the late 1880s, Aspen was a clapboard sprawl of hotels and slapped-up shanties, ready to eclipse Leadville as a boom town for silver. Its evenings offered a full array of saloons, cribs, music halls, and even an opera-comique that doubled as a roller rink. But Aspen lacked that monument to refinement and sophistication that alone could elevate a mining town from lust and materialism — an opera house. No matter that Aspen also lacked a hospital; what Aspen needed was a sugar daddy to provide culture. To that end one of the Smuggler Mine Company's major stockholders imported Jerome B. Wheeler, a director of Macy's in New York.

Wheeler's motives were financial, and what he raised was a commercial building on its first two floors. A bank, a haberdashery and a Ladies' Palace of Fashion fronted the street; the second floor was filled with offices for doctors, lawyers and the headquarters of the Aspen Mining and Smelting Co.; and only a 54-step stairway on the building's flank led to the crowning opera house. As architect Wheeler hired a man named Edbrook who had already built several major opera houses, including one in Denver for silver magnate Horace Tabor. Working with local sandstone in a Romanesque revival style, so intent was the architect on preserving symmetry that he continued the arched windows of the third floor to the area behind the stage, where they were non-functional and had to be boarded on the inside. Ground was broken in June, 1887, and the building was ready to open in April, 1888, then — and still — the tallest building in town.

The opera's interior won the public from the beginning. Enfolding the space like arms, and offering the best view, is the low, gracefully curving mezzanine with its continuously flowing wooden railing. Boxes project from either side of the proscenium, facing the audience more than the stage and complementing the mezzanine's curves. Most of the interior was accomplished with native materials, but morocco leather seats and chandeliers from the East gave the classic opera house touch, while an olio curtain depicting the six-year-old Brooklyn Bridge heralded the future. The curves of the stage apron, the boxes and the mezzanine created intimacy and a curious sense of rounding the square, leading a local critic to exclaim after the opening that the Wheeler was "a perfect bijou of a theater."

The spur line of the Midland and Rio Grande Railroads that took out ore for refinement now brought back shows for the refinement of citizens. But it must not be imagined that the Wheeler staged Grand Opera. Shows were odd precursors of the musical comedy and the disaster movie — pastiches of vaudeville and burlesque, with floods and fires on stage, heroines on treadmills, and an occasional plot line connecting some two dozen scenes and hundreds of costumes. Most shows were booked by a Denver agency referred to as the Silver Circuit and run by Baby Doe Tabor's brother. Loftier presentations included James O'Neill in *The Count of Monte Cristo* and Polish actress Modjeska in *As You Like It;* broader efforts sported horses on stage and, once, a small elephant that had to be belly-banded and hoisted from the outside. Stores advertised fashions for openings,

seamstresses received dress commissions, hands in kid gloves held unnecessary pearl-handled spy-glasses, and ladies were offered white silk programs with perfumed sachets. The Wheeler's opener, *The King's Fool,* so enchanted miners with its fencing team of eight Viennese ladies that they got up a purse for a local architect and amateur fencer. The next evening the architect challenged the lead fencer to a duel on stage, slashed her arm, bandaged her gallantly and handed her the purse. Between spectacles the Wheeler manager booked moral lectures for gentlemen only. If Aspen could boast such culture, it was no mere cul-de-sac.

Yet even as the opera house opened Aspen could see rough times ahead, and with the demonetization of silver in 1893 Aspen became what it most feared — a commercial and artistic dead end. Shrunk to a few hundred souls, the town took over the Wheeler and turned it into a community theater, staging their own musicals, maintaining the moral lectures for gentlemen, and presenting high school graduations. An elderly Aspenite still remembers being taken by her father to the Wheeler to see "the flickers." By 1912 the Wheeler had been acquired by a Texas businessman, and two mysterious fires occurred in one week. The entire town rushed to put them out, but gone were the stage floor, the olio curtain, the fourteen sets of scenery hand-painted by the scenic artist of the Chicago Opera. No one could prove the obvious: that the fires had been set for insurance. Blackened, water-damaged, heaped with debris, the Wheeler entered a dark age, a sealed cavern that overhung such ventures as a grocery, a library, a pub, a thrift shop.

The opera house, with Aspen itself, returned to life after World War II with the arrival of Chicago industrialist Walter Paepcke. Aspen's very isolation was an advantage in Paepcke's eyes, and he envisioned an ideal community where a combination of athletics, intellectual pursuits and the arts could produce his version of the Whole Man. Under his supervision the Aspen Skiing Corporation put the town on its financial feet, the Aspen Institute for Humanistic Studies convened the powerful and brilliant for intellectual exchange, and the Music Associates of Aspen put on the summer music festival. His friends Igor Stravinsky and Bauhaus designer Herbert Bayer cast covetous eyes on the Wheeler.

By 1947 the Wheeler had been mucked, cleaned and patched to the point that it could offer concerts by Burl Ives, radio broadcasts by Lowell Thomas, and at last what it had been destined for all along — Grand Opera. French composer Darius Milhaud became a festival composer-in-residence for the remainder of his life, and his wife

Madeleine Milhaud staged new works by her husband as well as standards from the repertoire. Current members of the music faculty still remember carrying the aging Milhaud, corpulent and confined to a wheelchair, up the 54 steps to his world premières.

In 1960 the Wheeler was remodeled on a modest but organized basis by Herbert Bayer. The Bauhaus of his origins rebelled against all Victorian excess, but Bayer achieved a synthesis by emphasizing existing lines with heavy black bordering, and adorning red walls with gold fleurs-de-lys. Movie seats were installed downstairs, wooden benches served the mezzanine, and the box seats became extensions of the stage. By no means a Victorian restoration, Bayer's remodeling was an interim step in the Wheeler's resurrection.

It was the Music Associates of Aspen that provided the catalyst for full restoration. With headquarters on the second floor and a desire for more dressing rooms, an orchestra pit, seats without loose springs, and some reassurance about fire, they offered $1/4 million as seed money. Community art groups were consulted for their needs, so that the Wheeler could be useful during the other three seasons. The City of Aspen raised the rest of the $4 1/2 million through a real estate transfer tax, whereby 1/2 of 1% of all real estate transactions within city limits went into a fund for the renovation and maintenance of the Wheeler.

With the appropriations came matching controversy. A sequence of task forces appointed by city council displayed the acrimony that enlivens Aspen politics. The architectural firm of William Kessler and Associates, Detroit, was appointed to design the renovation, and quickly clashed with the town. Architects objected, for instance, to the inclusion of a flown movie screen, while films at the Wheeler had become a local institution. The architects also wanted to retain benches in the mezzanine, and had to be prevailed upon to install chairs. The flash point occurred when the architects wanted to add backstage and dressing room space by appending a modernistic curving wing to one side. As soon as an architectural rendering appeared in *The Aspen Times*, the angry letters flew, returning architects to the drawing board. Adding background noise were politicians who simply thought the restoration a waste of money.

Meanwhile, the Wheeler was listed on the National Register of Historic Places, and certain regulations had to be observed. The original theater, for instance, never had an orchestra pit, and one for 46 musicians had to be designed so that it could be made to disappear when not in use. This was solved in a double fashion that permitted a thrust stage to advance over the pit, or for extra seating to close the same terrain. The original Wheeler never had a lobby, and space was created on the second floor by knocking out old offices. Most townsfolk expected the lobby to be decorated in the Victorian manner, and were outraged that the architectural firm came up with a spare modernistic design. It had to be explained that because the space itself was not original, historic designation required that the style be dissimilar enough to mark it off from what was authentic.

Public confidence hit bottom when a side wall was dismantled so that it could be rebuilt fifteen feet further out, and a major chunk near the top unexpectedly dropped to the ground. "It looked like it had been shot with a cannonball," remarked Wheeler Opera House Executive Director Robert Murray, and rumors flew through town that this time the restorers had really done it — the entire building was collapsing. Unfazed, the restoration crew kept at it for 2 1/2 years, nearly three times as long as it took to build it in the first place. Rows of dressing rooms were installed on two floors, as well as a large service elevator that would have been appreciated by the poor hoisted elephant. A more elegant public elevator was added in front. Functional improvements included roof repairs, sprinklers, a new boiler, a ventilation system, and two sets of fire stairs in back.

It was in the restoration of the décor that the greatest care was lavished. By chemical analysis of paint scrapings, original colors were duplicated. The Victorians tried to simulate building materials so that plaster looked like stone and plain wood took on grain. Faithful to this falsification, panels were grained by painters with toothbrushes, and plaster over brick was scored to resemble stone blocks. Seating proved less feasible to duplicate. As Americans have broadened in the beam, theater owners have constantly had to widen their seats. Morocco leather proved too expensive and difficult to maintain, and because of comfort and fire regulations, the single center aisle had to be replaced with two side aisles. But the red plush fabric, fire retardant and good for acoustics, gives the same richness, and cast-iron end-standards add authentic trim. The olio curtain of the Brooklyn Bridge was repainted from old designs. Of the total vibrancy of colors, Robert Murray says, "You'd wince at the idea — there's hot Polish pink, electric blue, orange, battleship grey, and scarlet carpets, but the Victorians knew how to pull it off with panache."

When the renovated Wheeler opened on May 24, 1984, disputes disappeared as if through a trap door. The 502-seat theater upstaged the show, and patrons were reassured even by the spacious, contemporary second floor lobby when they saw that it sported an angled bar where they could gather, and that the walk-in safe had been converted into a champagne closet. Even penny-pinching politicians added their approval when they heard the comments and read the ecstatic press. The generous dollars and short fuses had all been worth it.

Since the Wheeler's Grand Opening it has been booked solidly, with a wider spectrum of events than in its previous nine decades. The summer music festival has expanded its program of opera, chamber concerts and master classes, and during the rest of the year the stage has hosted dance programs, foreign films, benefits, jazz and rock concerts, weddings, and most popular of all, the annual fall musical staged by Aspenites. Members of Moses Pendleton's dance troupe Momix debuted two experimental pieces incorporating video, strobe and rear screen projection, and Lily Tomlin spent five weeks in the winter of 1985 perfecting the one-woman show she took to Broadway. A street-level sales office coordinates tickets to Wheeler events and most other cultural events in the valley. A staff of volunteers supplements the salaried employees, and its integration with the town insures that Aspen's cultural life doesn't fold with the music tent at the end of August. A kind of summation of all its previous careers, the Wheeler will soon celebrate its hundredth birthday looking like the newborn.

23.

Ki Davis: The Mysteries Remain

The passing of Ki Davis in January, 1983, not only deprived Aspen of one of its most vibrant personalities, but cut off a deepening vision in no less than three of the arts. Ki's collage, always striking, increasingly gathered its harmonies around a powerful central mass. The poetry, begun later and doubtless farther from its eventual destination, was expanding in range. A career in sculpture, begun in the last few years, was triumphant from the beginning. Beyond the personal loss, a terrible sense of incompleteness hovered about the death by cancer of this 57-year-old woman — a sense strong in my own life when I arrived at the apartment of an ex-Aspenite in New York ten months later.

My friend had moved back to the city after several years in Aspen, and the work of Aspen artists hung on her walls. "There's more," she said, after I toured the rooms. "There's a collage by Ki Davis, probably the strongest piece in her last show, and I bought it when there was a rage to buy Ki's stuff. But it seems death-obsessed, and I really don't want to hang it. I'm not sure what to do with it."

"May I see it?"

It was certainly large and dark, composed primarily of two kinds of black paper, one glistening and one dull, with bits of other colors grouped around the central shape that characterized her last phase. Yes, my friend would sell it, for the price she paid for it. Removed from its gallery frame and swaddled in packing material, it was the most cumbersome hand luggage I ever wrestled onto a plane.

But what, actually, had I bought? The ragged horizontal figure that dominates the picture is of a strange material indeed — a pulpy black paper shiny as anthracite and cross-hatched with reinforcing threads that continue, beyond the paper's torn borders, in loose hairs. Bleached randomly into greys and buffs, it looms from a rectangle of matte black paper, spilling over its borders as if blooming from a night sky. Scattered upon it and fixed to its sides are scraps of paper the color of sandstone, bits of indigo, a lone fleck of red. Because of the proliferation of dark texture and detail, the collage is best seen with your nose right up to it, at a distance less than the work's own width.

There is no deciphering what in particular was meant, but I have asked Ki's husband, John Davis, what he knows about the piece. He told me that Ki found the paper in a field outside Boulder while he was there on business, and that the paper was already black and apparently made for packaging. Ki peeled it open, found the strange texture inside, and got very excited. She built two collages around it, the other of which is in the collection of a corporation in Illinois. The deep blue is placed so as to suggest sky, yet I feel I am looking down on something: this is a species of map-making, the folds and fault blocks of a mythical country. Black is more than the color of death; it can suggest power, elegance, even a kind of glamor. There are no shades of black, insists a purist friend. Here is proof to the contrary.

Before I saw Ki's work, collage struck me as a hobbyist's art, paste-up for those without the discipline or the vision to wield a chisel or a brush. Most of it still strikes me that way. But from the first glance, Ki's work seemed possessed of a single voice, elusive but personal. That voice, it turns out, was well trained. A native of Tacoma, Washington, Ki majored in art at Scripps College, and became the first person to earn a masters in painting at the University of Illinois. She had one-person gallery shows in Aspen and Chicago, and was included in group exhibitions at the Art Institute of Chicago, the Santa Fe Museum, and numerous colleges and universities. She considered drawing the basis of the visual arts, taught drawing in the Chicago area, and held life drawing classes after her move to Aspen in 1973. Her career as artist and teacher continued unabated through the raising of five children. When she turned to collage — or when it ran away with her — she wound up making much of her own paper, and didn't hesitate to apply effects with ink, charcoal, watercolor, or even spray paint if the piece called for it.

For Ki, then, collage represented no lack of discipline, but like her other two arts, it was fired by intuition. Showing a poem, she would say, "Isn't it wild? — I have no idea where it came from," her voice both proud and a little frightened. Her character embraced such contradictions. Slender, delicate of feature, with a quiet and oddly transparent manner of speech, she seemed at once earthy and not quite attached to the earth. Her art grew from the same paradox, and she trusted the work to have meaning even when it resisted explanation. Our century has specialized in creation from the unconscious, ever since we decided we had one; the psychic core has become the credited source of our best recent art, as well as the alibi for most of our worst. It takes an artist like Ki to remind us that, beyond all fashion, to create a work of art one does not understand — or to be the agent of its creation — takes a kind of bravery.

To sense where Ki's art was headed, one has only to compare a late collage with previous work. By happy chance I also came by an earlier piece. Ki had asked to borrow some records and I offered her a stack of favorites. A year later she confessed, with embarrassment, that my records had gotten mixed up with hers and she no longer knew which was which: would I accept a collage in their place? I could easily have pulled my own records, but I leapt at the exchange. The piece she brought was a bright arrangement of browns and yellows, semi-representational, suggesting four oddly-shaped ceramics on a tabletop. It is harmonious, decorative, and particularly clever in suggesting the glazes of ceramics by the placement of stains inherent in the paper. And a stranger, seeing it next to the night vision, could sense immediately the chasms of experience that fell between.

Ki is perhaps best known in Aspen for her sculpture "Interplay," at the east end of the Hyman Street Mall, created from the small wax model with which she won the mall sculpture contest only a year after taking up sculpture itself. Another sculpture and several collages are on permanent display at Aspen Valley Hospital. That is only the public fraction of what she has left the town, and it is with a pang of recognition that a Ki Davis collage will suddenly leap out from a previously unseen wall — a pang, because the pleasure in the work is so mingled with the sense of someone extraordinary who slipped beyond us before she was fully revealed. It is characteristic of her that when I unwrapped the collage I brought back from New York, nearly a year after her death, I found a gummed label on the inside of the cardboard backing on which she had, in fact, given the work a title. It is called "The Mysteries Remain."

24.

Apparition

A small emerald clarity lost in granitic rubble, backed by 2000 feet of burnished granite, Capitol Lake might have been my favorite local waterhole in any case. A friend and I, both converts to Aspen, had been greedily exploring the lakes and passes of the Maroon-Snowmass Wilderness Area, and we reached Capitol Lake through the furious golds of the aspens on a mid-September day in 1963. Above timberline creation sparkled, then drained of color as clouds of burnt silver massed over the rocks. There were no other hikers and the day, like the lake itself, seemed in suspension. After lunch we climbed the pass beyond the lake, peered into Avalanche Basin, then started tiredly home. As we returned past the lake it began, gently, to rain.

Stumbling among the rubble, I stopped to catch my balance and glanced in the water. Just offshore, under perhaps six feet of water, lay a complete deer, jade green, flawlessly preserved. I gasped, then my friend saw it too. We gaped at a shared hallucination. But there was no doubting its reality: a two-pointer, its antlers tipped toward our feet, its flesh, apparently sealed by the icy water, clinging in folds and furred with a soft green algae. It was as if a bronze statue had tipped into the water and corroded. "You're going to take a picture?" whispered my friend, as if it were nearly morbid to raise the camera. We waited breathlessly the next ten days for the roll to come back.

I am the last holdout for stereo photography, a system briefly popular in the Fifties. The stereo camera takes two images at once, through lenses the same distance apart as the human eyes, producing a double slide which is resolved in the viewer. The effect is a deep window on the past, in full dimension, a square of life inviting the eyes to plunge — but only one pair at a time. The fad peaked and passed because party-goers, at first stunned by the depth, were then annoyed to hear one guest exclaim while ten more awaited their crack at the viewer and it took an hour to get through a dozen slides. Kodak, trying for twenty years to phase out its mistake, keeps raising the mounting charge, but I still hang on — largely because of the deer. As the viewer reconstructs it, the animal lies cradled among rocks whose slate is deepened to violet by water stopped like clear gelatin. A few raindrops form concentric rings on the lake's surface, which play in oval shadows over the deer's hide. Blooming out of the dark as if through a glass-bottomed boat, the image is beautiful but disturbing: an apparition.

How did the deer get there? Oldtimers — Johnny Herron, Mike Magnifico — were consulted. None had heard of such a thing, but all had theories. Perhaps it had fallen through the ice the previous winter. Perhaps a hunter had shot it while it was drinking at the edge, propelling it forward. Perhaps a hunter even pushed it in to avoid packing it out. The scenarios were all possible, but not very convincing.

A young visitor from Indiana, who sold tickets for Eastern Airlines and had never before seen the mountains, suggested that perhaps the deer was swept in by an avalanche. I examined my shots from the opposite side of the lake, and found the deer to be lying beneath avalanche slope. The answer will never be known, but that flatlander produced the likeliest theory.

How long had the deer lain there? I liked to imagine it frozen for years unnoticed, had no way of knowing except by projection backward, and returned the next summer to see if it remained. Indeed it did. But the water had dropped fifteen feet, turning it to a pale skeleton. Assuming the water dropped yearly to that level, the deer was the vision of a season. I placed the skull in the water, shot a few eerie if contrived stereos, then brought home the jawbone.

While I make no general claims for great photography, the slide of the deer has haunted enough people that I have laid in a supply of prints, and when asked for a copy I can — surprise! — pull one from a drawer. But stereos, for all their uncanniness in the viewer, enlarge badly. Fortunately, the image has appealed as well to artists. A friend in Monterey turned out a surreal if unsuccessful version in oil on masonite. My mother has produced a much finer rendition in water-color, which has the accuracy but not the hardness of a vast Kodak enlargement. It would be curious, in fact, to commission a series of distinguished artists to create their own versions — a project which (like my scheme to mount *The Rite of Spring* on skates) will succumb for lack of funds.

Since 1963 the image has gathered some minor addenda. When I spent several years out of the country, I lent my mother's painting to folksinger Katie Lee, who had former Aspen artist Irv Burkee frame it in barnwood. The nonreflecting glass, which my mother usually scorns for its dulling effect on color, in this case heightens the illusion of water. Recently a friend sent me a postcard from Finland with a drawing from the Peer Gynt legend — an aerial view of a reindeer with rider, sailing over a fjord — which bears an eerie resemblance. The jawbone has since been devoured by a house-guest's dog, but photograph, postcard and painting form a kind of collage around my desk, while a peek at the original through the viewer remains the climax of my house tour. And the memory of that initial vision at Capitol Lake will continue to haunt like one of those icons, jarring and strange, whose last meaning resists the light.

25.

A Landlord Speaks Out

Whoever rents out his personal living quarters for the first time will feel caught in a sudden freefall — denied familiar supports, displaced more centrally than if he were merely traveling, unsure whether he will light on the same earth. On the other hand, the prices one can command for a base camp in Aspen are a little hard to refuse, particularly if one has to pay off the house in question, and one becomes that nastiest of capitalists, the landlord. Once the threat has been survived, and banked, it is simply another strand in one's life, full of anxieties, risks, crises, moments of enlightenment, and rewards that are, surprisingly, not always monetary.

I began in the classic manner with a two-week Christmas rental, to a party I acquired through folksinger Katie Lee. The most prominent mortician from a small Arizona town would be arriving with a party of 24, to be equally divided between Katie's small house and my own. I couldn't conceive of a dozen people in my three modest rooms, but they assured me they had sleeping bags and were mutually compatible. The day before they were due an advance party arrived in the person of the mortician's son, who unloaded an entire commissary from his station wagon. Into my living room came gallons of wine, cases of beer, jumbo bags of popcorn and potato chips, hamburger buns, family-paks of cereal, loaves of Holsum Bread, plus sufficient plastic utensils and paper plates to outfit a Baptist picnic. I was, at the time, running the Aspen Recycling Center, was keenly conscious, deeply resentful, of Waste, and here was the enemy, heaped on my very hearth. Even the packaging, with its glossy reds and screaming yellows, seemed to hurl insults at the browns, tans and earth tones of my log walls.

In subsequent years I managed to leave as soon as renters arrived, but that winter I was playing piano for a melodrama called *The Drunkard,* inscrutably held over from the previous summer, and I moved into a friend's house across town. The day they arrived my renters invited me to cocktails in my own home, then dinner on the town. My house was unrecognizable, crammed with two dozen shrill, obstreperous Zonies, as Arizonans have become known, elders on bourbon and branch, youngsters belting their tourist Coors, the air marbled with cigarette smoke, the voices thunderous. Soon we piled into station wagons and invaded the Mother Lode, where a U-shaped table had been set up for our party in the back room. One of the women had a voice that you imagined could shatter plastic, and the others screamed to be heard over her. Carafes of house red were downed and the din rose. At that point the Mother Lode was considered cheap and loud by Aspen standards, but our room was aimed like a speaker at the rest of the restaurant, and we became the first party actually told to keep it down because people in the other rooms couldn't talk. I knew I shouldn't drink so much before playing the piano, particularly on the first night of our run in Snowmass, but the mortician kept splashing wine into my glass. I had been told that on occasion my piano playing saved the show, but that night my playing sank it. I had entered the world of landlords.

That traumatic first rental did the house no serious damage, and I spent subsequent Christmas rentals with family and friends in Phoenix, found I liked the change more than I missed skiing, and by gradual extension became an absentee for the entire winter. The first few full-season renters were local business people rather than visitors, and they expressed their personalities in the way they left the house. One renter kept changing her hair color and style, as well as modes of dress, and admitted without offense that I sometimes looked right through her on the street. She left a house in which cords no longer reached, plugs had the wrong number of prongs, lids were too large or too small for pots, the TV cable no longer screwed into the set. It seemed of a piece with her personal discontinuities and I began to think of her as Our Lady of Disconnections. I asked a waitress and two waiters sharing the house to put things back where they found them — meaning that they weren't to leave heavy furniture in strange places as other renters had done — and found exactly the same towels on the racks, utensils in the same order in the drawer, pillows arranged in my own pattern on the sofa, as if they had memorized my eye rather than my house. The next renter was less meticulous. Facing a move from my house to New York, she hired professional packers without having pre-sorted my possessions from hers. The packers kept asking what should stay and what should go. She complied at first, then snapped, "Don't bother me, just do it!" I returned to find I had inherited a lovely Chinese porcelain bowl, but half of my own favorites were missing. I stayed with her a few months later in New York. As I went through boxes she still hadn't unpacked, her sister dropped in from New Jersey and mentioned she was looking for the top to a ceramic Melitta coffee pot. "I happen to have one in the next room," I said, and fetched one from my pile.

"Do you *travel* with these things?" she asked.

"Ask your sister."

Not all local renters were business people. Most memorable was an artist we will call Lunette, who lived elsewhere in the valley and rented my place for a getaway studio and party house in town. Lunette came from a sumptuous background, received the income from familiar household products, and knowing she would understand how to care for them I left a few items of value I would have stashed from other renters, principally a pair of small Oriental rugs that pass for family heirlooms. Lunette reported she was thrilled with the house and it was too bad I was missing the parties. She shared my obsession with magpies, was feeding them hamburger on the deck, and offered to paint a huge one on the front door. She did tend to forget that checks were due in the middle of the month. I would send her little reminder notes like, "Beware the Ides of March," and usually had to follow them up with phone calls. The checks they would elicit were suitable for framing. On one the Aspen Country Day School had been crossed out and my name scrawled above, with the numbers clearly fudged. The bank in Phoenix said they'd run it through, but not to expect any money if Lunette didn't call her bank to assure them it was real. When I called Lunette, she explained she was down to her last check, realized too late the rent was due, and decided the house was more pressing than her son's tuition. On another occasion she sent me an invitation to the opening of her show, an 8 by 11 page of art folded and stapled once, inside of which were a half-dozen loose scraps of paper with quotations about art from such sources as Ruskin and Andy Warhol, plus a rent check. How all of these items arrived intact, open on three sides, is still unexplained, but I called Lunette to tell her I loved the package and had only one criticism: she'd signed the art but not the check.

When I returned, more of the story came out. She was visited for several weeks by a cousin whose writing I was dimly aware of, and whose diary was published annually. His publisher would not stand for a day in which nothing happened, and to get material they rounded up the most curious specimens on the mall, invited them over for the evening, plied them with booze, tolerated their dope, and observed them until 4 a.m., when Lunette frisked them for stolen books as they filed out the door. Still more emerged when I had the Orientals cleaned. While it didn't show from above, someone had pierced them with nail holes, said the rug cleaner, and they had lost hundreds of dollars in value. Lunette then admitted having nailed them to the wall to create a gypsy effect.

Lunette asked if she could rent again next year and divide the rent with her nephew, and was shocked when I agreed: no one had ever rented to her twice. I figured that I knew how to guard against her particular madness, knew what to hide and, besides, her nephew might be a stabilizing influence. I rented to them as a pair, then to her nephew alone, and the house sustained only minor damage. But I was wrong about the stabling influence of the nephew, for when I was cleaning in his wake I found a flyer that showed Ralph Steadman's drug-crazed caricatures from the front cover of Hunter Thompson's *Fear and Loathing in Las Vegas,* and a text that read, "Fear and Loathing in Aspen, A Savage Journey — Come Thanksgiving and Party thru New Year's, Aloha" — beneath which appeared a small map showing three locations: the Castle Creek Bridge, the Jerome Bar and my house. It was, of course, a landlord's coronary, softened only by the fact that the dates had safely passed. Lunette, meanwhile, left drawings for an opera to be staged in my house, including an aria from Act II called "We Share But One Heart," in which a couple in magpie costumes are about to bite into a suspended heart.

There was only one other party that I rented to for as long as three years, a friend's friend whom I never managed to meet. He had realized his ambition to retire at age forty, and spent his life sailing between Pacific islands. I thought of his party as my boat people. Because they were due to arrive after I left, I installed a friend who had just built a new roof, and who promised to clean the house and make minor repairs in return for staying there in the interim. They kept postponing the date and my friend kept postponing his cleaning. One day well after New Year's they announced they would show up in a few hours. Caught off guard, my friend rallied a companion and they threw themselves into a cleaning frenzy that, they insisted, spared no square inch. My renter thought otherwise and sent me a letter that stated, among other things, "You bought the shelf paper that was not used, you bought the light bulbs that were not put in, you bought the vacuum cleaner that was sparsely used.... Your house was a filthy mess, dead mice, spiders and flies all over, dirt everywhere." I flew into a rage and called my friend for an explanation. He assured me that the house was in order but my renters were anal retentives. Meanwhile, would I please inform them that he was my temporary house-sitter, not my vicar in Aspen, and would they quit calling and ordering him around.

So much for openers. My 26 shelves of books, by their count, would have to be cleaned or else "we can live with it by using air fresheners to cover the dusty, musty smell." Books to me smell as pleasant as lilies of the valley but then I don't live at sea, and we wound up hiring my renter's sister-in-law to purge them at a nominal hourly rate. They then reported that they had taken down the picture of the dead lamb and tucked it away. I explained that it was a painting by my mother of a deer I had found perfectly preserved in an alpine lake, and sent them an article I'd written about it for *Aspen Magazine*. They replied that it was an interesting story, nicely turned, but they had installed a bed in the studio and didn't want to lie there looking at a dead animal.

Things got serious when the bedroom ceiling collapsed. It had been a heavy year for snow, requiring them to shovel off the roof while missing the World Cup Downhill, and still snow had melted through the new shingles, refreezing in the crawl space and weighting the ceiling so that it sagged 18 inches in one corner. The captain of the boat people propped up the ceiling with a two-by-four, but would I contact my roofer to see if the leak could be plugged? The roofer was, of course, the notorious house-sitter, who couldn't believe he was resummoned. More shoveling and some patching eased the situation, but each side kept updating me on the latest while referring to the opposition as the wastrel or the anal retentives.

At the end of the winter the boat people asked if I'd like a copy of the log they kept while they were in the house. By all means, I said, thinking it might add to the lore of deer and owl sightings, interesting drop-ins and the like. A few entries will give the flavor:

> 1/20 *Garbage disposal does not work. Pipe to drain clogged solid. Cleaned iron pipe, replaced others. As we were taking showers after fixing drains, shower head broke. Not too good a day.*
>
> 2/24 *Phone won't work, order new unit.*
>
> 3/3 *Roof in bedroom came down, braced it up.*
>
> 3/18 *Received about the 10th call for Lunette. Who is this Lunette?*

On a ship there is little margin for imperfection, and it was probably courting trouble to install seafarers in a cabin where leaks are unrecognized until the vessel is actually sinking. But despite having been the magnet for more household disasters than all previous renters, the boat people assured me that they considered the house their home on land, and wanted to keep renting. Before the ceiling was repaired Lunette dropped by and suggested I leave it that way and allow her to carve the two-by-four into an Art Nouveau totem pole, but I knew the boat people wouldn't go for it. Inasmuch as the financial dealings and house care were both impeccable, I was anxious to keep them as renters. I also wanted to know whether to believe the wastrel or the anal retentives about the state of the house on their arrival, and next year instead of installing a house-sitter between my departure and their arrival, I cleaned in my own usual fashion and left a note saying they might find the house a bit dusty. I got a note from the captain saying that he had arrived two days early to muck up and found there was nothing to do — satisfying my curiosity. They used their non-recreational hours to design a new boat to take them around the world, and during their last season they asked if they could buy me a new and larger refrigerator. While I was proud of my 1947 Frigidaire that had never missed a beat in forty years, I accepted.

Whatever the care, one always returns to some unpredictable touch. I rented once to the proprietor of a failed laundromat in Snowmass and came back to a carport full of washing machines. Another time there was no trace of the key to the storeroom. I phoned the renter and was told, as if belaboring the obvious, that it was in the barbecue. I lifted the lid of the portable barbecue and there on the grill was the key. Another time I found a scrap of paper in the bathroom that read, "Patrice, I *can't believe* you would leave dirty sanitary napkins on the floor for other people to throw away!" I, in turn, couldn't believe Patrice's mother would leave such a note for me to find and, worse, publish.

Over the years I would say that the agony and the entertainment have balanced each other out, leaving the money. By now the mechanics of clearing way for renters — of storing what's vulnerable and subtracting my personality as represented in knickknacks — have become so routine that it seems a normal part of packing. If I have escaped some of the disasters I've heard of from other landlords and ladies, it may be because I always tried to rent to friends, or acquaintances of friends. Renters will be less likely to abuse a house if they know the tale will come back to haunt them, though a few free spirits — Lunette and her nephew spring to mind — are beyond such constraints. I have also tried to keep the rent slightly below market value, so renters won't revenge themselves over feeling ripped off. So far none of them have. Some have left their artwork as well as their gouges on the wall, and fielding their complaints by phone and by mail is one more way of consoling myself over being away, and of enjoying Aspen *in absentia*.

26.

Og's End

I felt fortunate that during the first years of owning a house in Aspen I was accompanied by a German shepherd who seemed three steps ahead of reality. A veteran of Cannery Row and three years in Spain, master of commands in four languages, Og had once beaten his way out of a dog pound located in the middle of a Spanish slaughterhouse, liberating the other dogs as well. Even as I tried to repress a sense of his superiority, as we marched to the post office I would hear a stranger behind me remark to another, "Look at that dog — he's really on top of it!" or "That animal doesn't miss a thing." A woman I didn't know once swam up to me in the Glenwood Springs pool and said, "You know, your dog ought to run for mayor."

"He can't," I could only stammer, inwardly puffed up, "he lives in the county."

So a behavioral suppressant like the new leash law only fired his imagination. Aspen had always paid a dogcatcher, but dogs roamed around town like a counterculture, intent on private business, exploring by committee, adding a social dimension that touched only marginally with humanity, and the law tended to smile on any infraction less crass than rabies. Then condominiums rose, fresh enclaves broke up the valley, humanity condensed, the balance tottered and the net drew down. At first the repression ended at city limits, and my house was Main Street's toe in the county. Og behaved as if he had studied a zoning map, made his rounds discreetly, and sat over the line as if daring the dogcatcher to overstep his limit for the purpose of slapping on a lawsuit. But walks to the post office now demanded a lead. While his spontaneity did turn me into a maypole, he seemed to understand confinement's escape into style, a sort of prance that was his version of the jive walk, and when we reached the most savage corner he awaited the sign to proceed before it occurred to me to teach him that basic move. Once when I set down a bag of groceries to adjust his leash he calmly picked it up and carried it the rest of the way home, over a mile, ignoring a young cynic on a balcony who yelled, "You make him pay the rent too?" Thereafter, with a certain crusty importance, he automatically grabbed any bag up to four pounds, never once dropped one, and it was only my own lack of faith and the tendency of his saliva to rot even City Market's touted double-ply bags that prevented him from carrying the bottles of hot sauce, or the acquisitions from Uncle Willy's Spirit House.

But a reawakened urge to wander in his late career coincided with a periodic crackdown and he was nabbed, taken to a pound too fortified for the kind of escape he had led in Spain, held overnight, and I was stuck with my first genuine fine. This event recurred within the month, at doubled expense, and my attention was reached. I bought twenty yards of plastic cord and secured him in his own yard, an indignity which humiliated us both. Our reward for such purity was a slap in the face: a leather lead donated by an admirer snapped while he was tied downtown at an already embarrassing Doggie Hitching Rack and he was picked up on the spot. I returned from my errands, untied the remaining half and ran to the animal control truck, still visible only a block away. Og was protesting from the back in a fury, the other half of the leather dangling from his neck. I ran to the cab with my half. "That dog was *tied*. Please let him go."

"Sorry," said the eager new assistant dogcatcher. "The dog was loose. That is no longer legal."

Technically in the wrong, I felt persecuted. Og spent a night in jail, but rather than pay the fine I threw myself on the mercy of the court on grounds of intended virtue.

The case came up a month later under Judge Scott. I was not, I noted, the only irate dog owner, but protests of harassment were largely passed over. I sat through a slate of pet and parking infractions, took heart when a young man got his case postponed on grounds that the current moon was unpropitious, then my name was called and the assistant dogcatcher stated where and when he had captured Og.

"How do you plead, Mr. Berger?" asked Judge Scott.

I had listened closely to the judge's introductory remarks that possible pleas were guilty, not guilty, and *nolo contendere,* the latter "no contest" being an apparent acquiescence to conviction without actual admission of guilt. *"Nolo contendere."*

"Mr. Berger, no one has actually pled *nolo contendere* in this court. It is a legal technicality that really only applies at higher judicial levels, and here means the same thing as guilty. Would it be all right if we kept things simple and you just pled guilty?"

"All right," I swallowed. "Guilty."

"Do you have anything to say in your defense?"

"Yes." I held up my half of the lead. "My dog was attached with this. I realize that the dog was technically in violation by being loose downtown, but I would like the court to take into consideration that I did try to obey the law."

"Let me see the lead," demanded the judge.

I handed it to him and he looked at both ends. "In view of the obvious intent to comply with the law I am going to do something legally unprecedented. I am going to find someone innocent who has pled guilty."

"Your honor, I object!" The assistant dogcatcher leapt to his feet. "The dog was in clear violation. It is the duty of the owner to provide a lead strong enough to hold his dog. Besides," he added in an undertone, "I can prove that the lead didn't just happen to break. It was chewed off."

"Oh?" said Judge Scott.

"Yes," said the young man, advancing to the judge's table." I can prove it. If you will observe closely, here, here and here, you will see the tooth marks."

It was a revelation to me as well. The judge bent even closer, turned the lead in his hand, then looked up. "You are correct. The dog chewed his way out. While I wish to commend your zeal in the performance of your duty, I must remind you that it is people rather than animals that are being tried in this court."

The assistant dogcatcher, maintaining his poise through an afternoon of dog owners' complaints about himself, was near the end of his own rope. "Perhaps you could reduce, or even suspend, payment of the fine, without making a mockery of the law, a law I am paid to enforce at considerable peril, by finding the party innocent."

"No," persisted Judge Scott, "I am going to let Mr. Berger completely off the hook — Scott-free, as it were," and in the pall of a bad pun Og beat his last rap.

Og's surprising turns of mind, particularly toward the end of his life, occasionally exceeded the confines we usually ascribe to animals of higher intelligence, including ourselves. Part of an animal's sensitivity is doubtless his keen sense of pattern, the kind of specious cause and effect blown into cultural solutions by Skinner: Og noted, for instance, the abrupt way I avoided being caught downtown without a john by taking a perfunctory pee before our walks, and yelped in spirals of ecstasy whenever I voided in that manner. But Dennis, Og's owner and then co-owner, began to notice that Og, dozing near the dinner table, snapped alert not at the moment of being offered a bite, but just before, in the split second Dennis *thought* of it. It recalled, he said, nights during Og's puppyhood on a boat in the San Diego harbor when Og lay curled on the lid to the john and Dennis, lying motionless on his bunk and suddenly recognizing the need to go, would hear Og scramble politely to the floor. When discussed in his presence Og would begin to blink like Nixon and avert his eyes, but once during a visit my mother, sleeping in the study, felt something boring into the back of her skull in the middle of the night, and turned to find Og staring at her fixidly in a silent appeal to be let out. One friend became convinced that Og was posing as a German shepherd while filing his daily dispatch to Mars.

A late instance of his perception left me a little shaken. I usually left Og with devoted neighbors when I took off for extended camping trips. The routine became a standard collaboration: I carried his food in a bag and he carried his dish, an arc of pale green curving over his eyes as he trotted beside me, businesslike and blind. When I packed for whole seasons, springs in Baja, he would sprawl over as many square feet as possible, fending off the cargo; at the crestfallen moment when the car had been packed by yelling him away and the door closed without him, a light went out of his eyes, his bearing sank, my heart crumpled, and by the time the car was half backed to pull away he was trotting to the neighbors' with what looked like a smile on his face.

It was an adaptation with which all parties were delighted until my neighbors' two sons were rebuilding their Volkswagen bus for a trip to South America. Lured by constant excitement and perhaps the hope of an invitation, Og lay on their corner all day, returned only at mealtime, then not at all. In lighter moments we placed sunglasses on his nose and he left them in place, glaring darkly at tourists who rounded the bend into town thinking that perhaps Aspen was even more sophisticated than they had feared. Yet gradually I felt annoyed, then seriously rebuffed, and when some friends of the adventurers inquired whether they were taking their dog, an anger welled within me, a possessiveness of which I had not been aware.

That evening while I was installed in the corner of the floor where I sip scotch and torture poems, a power spot if I have any, I summoned Og for a small conference. He regarded me with a certain attention. I explained that he was my dog, not the neighbors' dog, that he was not to spend his entire life on their corner, that he was not to shift his allegiance at this point, that my house was his and would remain so. I raved on without gesture, with no prop but the verbal abandon of the third scotch, but from then on Og never neared their house. The neighbors noticed it immediately. "What's come over Og?" they asked. "Suddenly he won't even say hello. He acts like he doesn't know us."

I remained silent, secretly awed. But I had only solved one problem to create another: they were still my dogsitters, and my next absence threw them into a panic. Og refused food from them, would not enter their house. He lay all day in the middle of the road, oblivious to traffic that skidded around him. They feared for his life. He grudgingly consented to eat outside and spend nights in their delivery van, surly with protest.

When I returned I tried to convey to Og that there was perhaps some middle ground: he could be friendly to them and make it up — without, of course, moving in — for their feelings were deeply hurt. But it was too late, or delivered too ambiguously, for his aloofness persisted to the end. I knew that Og had a vocabulary of several dozen words scattered through four languages, but refused to believe he had cracked English grammar. I do find it likely that many animals, including ourselves, grasp directly the projections that language so crudely abstracts, and await ethology and parapsychology to confirm levels of communication for which current evidence is all but statistical.

Having experienced Og in such plenitude as to make him seem virtually indestructible, it was hard to believe that the laws of canine mortality — so unkind in their ill-paired lifespans that cause feelings incessantly to be yanked by the roots out of humanity — could apply to a spirit so inexhaustible. Yet there was a perceptible slowing down, then an afternoon in his twelfth year when I walked out of the post office to find him staring glassily in the back of the car, a hind foot extended irrationally, unable to control his back motions. The vet diagnosed a mild stroke, showed me the fixed dilation in one eye, and cautioned me that Og could live another five years or be gone tomorrow. Og soon regained sufficient control of his muscles to grab the grocery bag, now walking a little sidestroke as he had always run, and that fall he accompanied a friend from Holland and me on an extensive tour of the West that turned out to be a farewell swing.

The following summer cut him swiftly, perhaps with more strokes, and by mid-August he could not walk at all. It was clearly the end, and not wanting him to suffer the agony our awareness of death vainly prolongs, I considered putting him to sleep. By the day of decision it felt like enlightened murder. I hoped he still might rally awhile longer and his evident lack of pain pled for a few more days. That afternoon he crawled into the study and seemed to ask to go out. I carried him to the juniper over Castle Creek where he often slept, and he lay curled for hours where I left him, oblivious of where he was, breathing with great deliberation.

I felt he could not survive being moved, but neither could his condition withstand the cold of an Aspen night, even in August, and by midnight, a moon retreating from the full between dense clouds and the ground thick with dew, I lifted him as well as I could in position and carried him into the house. Breath came so slowly that each seemed a momentous event, with such repose between that I thought each the last. An expression of disgust, as if of bad taste, played about his mouth. I rested a hand on his head, intending comfort, but he seemed so self-involved, his going so private, that my touch seemed an intrusion and I withdrew it. If life is vomit, I whispered, spit it out. After a few more massive breaths his legs stiffened, moved independently back and forth. There was a shot of mist to his eyes, and the lungs stilled. I buried him under the cottonwoods.

Despite the intensity of that moment it was a long time before his absence could be believed. I still woke in the night to his scratch on the door, returned from town braced for his leap, took my per-functory piss to expect him spinning and yelping with walk in his eyes. If he had learned my own movements, so I had learned his. Dogs and ourselves, goes the account, have woven our lives for mutual advantage, in symbiosis. If communication does exceed its outward sign, perhaps our common evolution is deeper than we have imagined. It wasn't until Og was gone that I realized that I had unknowingly sensed him at night, wandering the edge of the property common to us both like an extended dream, a liberated thought. A dog is perhaps more than a wakeful companion and a reliable buttress of human self-esteem, but is also an alien sensor on the fringe of a shared belonging, a ranging defense, an adept, an eye through the dark, securing and extending the dim edge of one's outmost consciousness.

Og's absence is, of course, confirmed, and there is no longer the sense upon opening the door to mere furniture that the house's heart has stopped beating. There is no mail for him now in the box, no long distance calls to wish him a Happy New Year. A few legends still return like weeds. They seem hardy enough in Aspen, and have relatives in many states, in England, Holland, and Spain. They bring back much that keeps falling from his owner's bad memory.

27.

A Tracker's Guide to Georgie Leighton

Even those who have never met Georgie Leighton — or who know the outspoken letters defending animal rights in local papers but have not matched them with a person — will exclaim, after the least clue, oh, *that's* Georgie Leighton. For those in such categories, Georgie Leighton is the sixtyish muscular woman, five-foot three, who can be seen powering her bicycle around town or on the perilous margins of Highway 82, her deeply tanned legs bared to all weather, pressing to mysterious destinations as if no force, human or trans-human, dared stop her. Georgie's is the voice, metallic, cascading with French *r's,* scarcely pausing for air, that rings through the post office in outrage that a nearly extinct breed of tortoise is being mindlessly poisoned in the Caribbean. Hers is the sun-bitten, craggy, squarish face under a cornice of close-cropped steel-grey hair, expressing energy like a coiled spring, animating a form so compressed it seems geological.

As if explaining the one dull species, she says, "I've never become good at anything. I have no money, no possessions, no clout. I belong to too many organizations. I have many gaps because I don't have a biological background. My memory keeps getting worse, and I start a book without realizing I've read it before. Everything I do is half-measure." Such modesty may be protective coloration, for she keeps meticulously ordered boxes of files, owns as extensive a library on animal behavior as her cramped quarters will allow, and claims to spend some eight hours a day researching threatened animals and firing off letters in their defense. Congressmen, for whom Georgie's issues are not a major source of votes, know her well enough to wish, in friendly postscripts, that she enjoy her next bicycle trip. Her respect for the academia she missed is equivocal enough that she can remark, of a biology instructor, that "he didn't have a degree, so his mind is not polluted." Contradiction is a mark of our species, but the route to Georgie's is more interesting than most.

Georgie was born in France, of a French father and a Swiss mother, a family that moved with the seasons, so that Georgie grew up half in Nice and half in Lausanne, on Lake Geneva. Her father began work as a "waterboy — today you would say busboy," and finally became a partner in a hotel. It was, she said, an earthy, middle-class childhood in the country, without electricity or indoor plumbing. To take a Saturday bath you closed all the gates around the courthouse, filled a wooden tub, stripped, and trusted your cousins' word that they wouldn't peek. One Saturday they let in the pigs, who chewed the soap and tried to join her in the tub. "I'm sure my cousins were watching," she says, "and laughing."

At a tender age she became interested in politics. Just as Americans throw away every section of the paper except the sports page, she says, in Europe everything gets tossed but the politics. The family had unshakable political beliefs, and her father's party gave her a bucket of paint and instructions to slap the party's number on the local walls. It was vandalism she enjoyed.

Her kinship with animals developed less rapidly. She remembers gazing out of an apartment at kids throwing rocks at a curly-haired terrier. She rushed down, and the dog that would let no one near it ran to her for protection. It was filthy and mangy, but in those days a veterinarian would treat only working animals and the family took it as it was. The family also acquired a tank of goldfish that wound up eating each other, and Georgie developed severe misgivings about fish. She remembers that as an adolescent she engaged in furious arguments with teamsters who goaded overworked horses into hauling carts of meat and beer up steep hills. On the other hand, she worked one summer for a slaughterhouse attached to a country butcher shop — a job that included killing heifers by hammering them on the head, hanging them, bleeding them, and cutting them into meat. "I was very strong when I was young, and could match any fellow working. What I was actually doing didn't strike me, because it was utilitarian. We certainly didn't have Safeways, with little things wrapped in plastic. You went into a butcher shop, the butcher shook off the flies, and you chose a cut of meat that got wrapped in a newspaper. I liked to do different things, and that job was one of them."

Her principal young obsession was neither politics nor animals. Nor was it the sea she grew up by but never much cared for, and that still smells to her like a Forest Service campground after a bad season. Her grand passion was the United States, and particularly the American West. She studied enough European history to get her through school, but treated cowboys and Indians more studiously — while admitting she wasn't above putting feathers in her hair. She read *Gone With the Wind* in translation. Her family had no relatives in the States, her father had turned down an offer to move there, and her mother didn't approve of a twenty-year-old daughter who lived in a fantasy of the Wild West. But her father accepted that she had been "hit over the head," and gave her yearning his blessing. It was just after World War II, French citizens had regained their homeland, and Frenchmen without family in America were not candidates for emigration at a time when Europe was swamped with refugees.

There began for Georgie two years of wandering through Europe that she describes as "the best years of my life, probably." Based primarily in Germany, she was employed by the United Nations to help locate relatives of concentration camp survivors. She escorted Jewish children by train to homes where they would be adopted. She assisted the Lutheran Church in helping refugees relocate and find jobs in the United States, adding that she avoided a similar program run by the Catholics because they so burdened it with restrictions and allegiances to dogma that had left bad memories from childhood. Fascinated with radio, she worked for Voice of America, and boasts that its parent organization, the U.S. Information Agency, would consult her before the *International Hearld Tribune* about American politics because they knew she made such a hobby of it.

Her real goal remained emigration to the United States, and with the help of a sympathetic employer she managed to obscure her French citizenship and be declared "stateless." She wrote to the *International Herald Tribune,* published in Paris, asking if any American family would be willing to sponsor her. The Leighton family was interested, but wanted assurance that she and not a ghostwriter had produced the fine letter in English. "I loved *Time Magazine,"* says Georgie, "and the English I aimed for was Timese." The Leightons were convinced, Georgie adopted their family name, and booked passage for the United States.

So anxious was she to begin life as an authentic American that she asked the ship's steward to bring her the same breakfast that the American officers were enjoying at the next table. She drank the milk, then nearly choked on the dry corn flakes. Without offending her self-esteem, one of the officers instructed her in how to apply milk and sugar to the flakes, then eat them "before they got dilapidated." Equally mystifying was her first bite of sweet potato: what was this dessert doing in the gravy? The Leightons greeted her warmly, then made the mistake of taking her to a drug store. Never having seen a revolving stool, Georgie wouldn't stop spinning and eating ice cream, then couldn't be pried from a rack of greeting cards, an innovation she had never imagined. Her favorite radio show became "Life with Luigi," so close was that parody of Italian immigrants to her daily experience.

She settled in Springfield, Massachusetts, worked as a file clerk for an insurance company, found the climate too cold, and enrolled in a radio school in Washington, D.C. She held a succession of radio jobs — in Maryland, in Washington, on both coasts of Florida — doing programming, research, bookkeeping, checking legal angles, scanning for dirty words, everything but announcing because she found background more exciting and also — she says with a laugh — "because of the French accent I would *still* like to lose."

She found the eastern United States very much like Europe, with houses close together, traffic heavy, and too little relief from one's kind. Still she made the most of it, taking up with friends her age who raced bicycles and hiked the Appalachian Trail. "We had a little Rambler, with four bikes wrapped in blankets in the back, and whenever we went through a toll booth I had to dive under because it was illegal to have four people in the front seat." During weekends in Maryland she would pedal through the District of Columbia into Virginia, where she visited with Arthur Godfrey's pet elephant. But her interest in politics was still primary. She got a pass to the Senate and House galleries, rode elevators up and down to see politicians up close, and felt frustrated as a resident of the District of Columbia that she had neither Senators nor a voting Representative. While working in a dime store, she called in sick and attended the McCarthy hearings. "Point of order! — I wouldn't have missed it." But it cost her a job when the camera panned the gallery and she was spotted by her boss. Constant changes of address delayed her becoming a citizen, but she estimates that when she took the test in 1956, she probably knew the American political system better than the examiner.

Gradually she extended her bicycle forays to the West of her childhood dreams, passing first through Aspen in 1959. She loved the mountain passes, particularly the tough work, the sheer sweat of pedaling uphill. Winding up in Aspen again in 1964, low on money, she was offered a job doing maid service. She quit her radio job in Washington and got rid of most of her belongings. Installed in Aspen, she worked as a maid, a clerk, a dishwasher, a checker in City Market — all the classic Aspen positions. "I'd thought of doing radio work here," she says, "but who wants to live in Aspen with a fulltime job?"

Crucial in Georgie's life were the six summers she spent at Elk Mountain Lodge, in Ashcroft. After her first summer there, camping in a tent, the owners asked if she would like to work as a wrangler during the fall. She had to learn horses quickly, she says, "how to tell the mane from the tail, to saddle and to put in the bit. I wound up falling desperately, hopelessly in love with a strawberry roan. I've never had so close a friend, and I still cry over him." He had been a rental horse, but because of Georgie's help at the lodge, the owners turned him over to her succeeding summers. Once they stayed out for six weeks, passing through Telluride and Durango, with Georgie in shorts breaking ground through snow for the horse, and the horse keeping his head behind Georgie to stay dry. The expedition marked the facets for which Georgie is best known: the spectacular adventures she undertook alone, and her brotherhood with animals.

It is her travels by bicycle that have been most legendary, consuming the summer months and taking her the length of Canada, or through convolutions drafted by whim. On the last and longest trip, in 1981, just under 10,000 miles, she dropped in on friends in Minnesota, Winnipeg and the state of New York. In Maine she officiated at bicycle races, explaining that she never raced herself, but was "the nut who stands on the sidelines with orange juice and spare wheels." She returned through the Deep South. "Oh, God, Louisiana, those subdivisions, they never end, in the swamps, everywhere, giant mosquitoes, and people shooting all the time. One night I slept in the middle of an old logging road, the only dry place I could find. Nobody drove by, and it was too dark even to poach, but there were bullets over my head in the pitch black. It was really too close for comfort. By the time I got to Kansas, my knee was so big it had swelled all the way to the ankle, and I was nearly passing out from the pain. From there I hitchhiked in a tiny plane that got me to Denver."

An Aspen doctor "who shall remain nameless" took x-rays, told her it was just old age, and there was nothing to do. Another operated, but would take no responsibility if she cycled again. She cycles still, only on the flat, but on bikes that deliberately fight back. "I'm a gear pusher," she says, "I *like* to work hard."

If cycling necessarily abated, her obsession with animals only increased. Summers with the strawberry roan led to an interest in wild horses and a friendship with the legendary Wild Horse Annie, scourge of Nevada ranchers who thought public lands were for cows. An interest in whales led to sea otters, to river otters, fur seals, harp seals, mountain lions, black bears. She read books, sent for monographs, joined protective organizations. She began attending semi-

143

nars: a course on raptors, a symposium on the blackfooted ferret. She traveled to see specific animals: the Minnesota wolves, the baby seals of the Magdalen Islands. Supreme were the courses on grizzlies — her favorite animal — and the time spent camping in grizzly country. "If it says grizzly, I'm there! But I wouldn't camp in grizzly country again because if there were an incident, I wouldn't want a grizzly killed on my account. If my overaged flesh can feed a grizzly, fine, but it would set a bad precedent. I do obey the rules, within reason."

Georgie's defense of endangered animals, for all its passion, has overtones of a professional operation. Information on various species is catalogued in four large boxes of files — except that the species are not arranged alphabetically or biologically, but in the order of Georgie's first interest in them. Almost daily come legislative updates and action alerts, and Georgie feels morally compelled to respond. She has a box labeled *Pending,* another labeled *To File,* and staples copies of her responses to initiating requests. An elaborate calendar documents letters to be written, statements acknowledged. She admires people, she says, who can focus on one issue, who can work for Friends of the Sea Otter without being distracted by red wolves, but there are too many species in trouble — how can one deny them help? But every organization depends on membership

144

dues and sends special pleas for donations. Each organization feels itself the most fiscally imperiled, the most crucially in need of statements, and they remind Georgie of high school teachers who feel their own assignments are the most important.

She would love to do more than write letters — to join an animal liberation group, to raid laboratories — but finds little support for such activism in Aspen. Supporters here pat her on the back, tell her she's doing fine, just keep it up. She envies a friend in Greenpeace whose active confrontations give her the release of doing something *bodily*. She especially admires friends in New York who spray-paint fur coats on the street, then slip into the crowd — tactics impossible in a hamlet like Aspen. "It's vandalism," she admits, perhaps recalling childhood brushwork for her father's political party, "but it gets the point across."

Her life, in any case, has not shrunk to deskwork. On her bicycle trips downvalley she collects roadkills, and was particularly delighted to find three fresh weasels between the airport and Shale Bluffs, which she cut into equal portions and fed to the wounded hawks being nursed at the Aspen Center for Environmental Studies, at Hallam Lake. She was especially enamored of an owl that had lost a wing, would hop toward her as she approached and click its beak. "When I got my dentures, the first thing I thought of was, now I can click back at the owl. I've never had such pretty teeth — I wish I'd had them when I was eighteen." Fascinated with animal scat, she has taken courses in scatology, and makes a hobby of studying samples from her collection. And while she never took up technical climbing, she has developed a taste for rappelling and dreams of someday rappelling out of a helicopter.

Georgie has survived her adventurous life with no injuries she considers serious, not even the time a terrified employer watched her fall off a hay wagon and hit her head on the ice with a terrifying shriek. It turns out that as a girl she had gotten free judo lessons by being the one the others got to throw, and the shriek was part of her technique for a relaxed fall. She attributes her health largely to an unsanitary childhood in the country. "Every bug on this earth tried to cut me down and finally gave up, because, knock on wood, I never get the flu, never get sick. I get dusty, but I don't consider it dirt. Also I saw my father work himself into the ground and die at age 62, and that was my inspiration — never overwork. I don't think I'm in any danger of that." Never a great meat-eater by American standards, ten years ago she became a vegetarian, and whatever orthopods warn, she considers daily cycling an investment in health. In 1968 she gave up smoking — but hardly for reasons currently fashionable. "I used to buy cartons of Pall Malls. I *enjoyed* smoking, and never worried. First thing in the morning you open your eyes, you light up that long cigarette of American tobacco, you inhale, let it drift and tickle your nose . . . Oh, God, it was heaven! But I had to be very frugal, had to choose, and finally decided I liked books more. I especially wanted the Charles Addams series, though now my favorite book is *Platero and I.*"

For all her exuberance, Georgie admits to moments of discouragement. For two decades in Aspen she has put up with the same menial jobs, the price she pays for disappearing every summer. But some jobs, such as clerking, have become more trying because of her awareness of the customers — not so much the hunters which, "in Aspen, you hardly notice unless you get a knucklehead walking around in an orange outfit with meat spoiling on his radiator" — but because of the difficulty of being civil to clientele wearing furs. At this point she prefers the relative insulation of, say, doing laundry for a condominium. For ten years, surrounded by Aspen abundance, she has lived in the same single basement room that contains her bed, her files, bookcases, skis, mementos and, in the winter, two suspended bicycles. She has no kitchen, cooks on a burner, and figures she spends more on postage than on food. Most discouraging of all, alas, is the animal rights movement itself, with species succumbing at an accelerating rate while the very issue, for now, is politically on the back burner. By moments she feels like giving up, but is prevented by her conscience, and also by organizations that keep you fired up so that politicians can't say they've gotten rid of you. Neither bad politics nor a bad knee have grounded her summers, however, for she merely takes the same expeditions by motorcycle, recently attending a wildlife conference in Boston, working off rent doing kitchen cleanup as a "senior youth hosteler," and chaining her motorcycle to a rabbit cage so that anyone who stole it would be stuck with the rabbits too.

As she reads these words, Georgie will likely be disappointed that I have chosen to speak merely about her, rather than the defenseless nonhuman sensibilities so desperately in need of public discovery. But Georgie, in one sense, represents more than herself — she has come to symbolize something about the town as well. By my own count, we have had in recent times three other such Aspenites: jazz clarinetist Freddie Fisher, Aspen's patron saint, or at least patron sinner; Fred Iselin, who merged Aspen's improbable skiing with his unlikely personality; and Ralph Jackson, Aspen's self-appointed court

146

jester. Georgie differs from these by being female and vibrantly alive, but unlike the others, all of whom weren't above trading on colorful personas they were aware of, Georgie also has a paradoxical reserve, and seems self-effacing about her own self-assertion — lest it get in the way of what she is trying to accomplish. All are gregarious, but Georgie faces beyond public perception, beyond her own species.

The same Georgie will seem to many an eccentric, a crank, a monomaniac, perhaps even a bore. To detractors one can offer only perspective. In the seventeenth century an influential French mathematician and philosopher named René Descartes assured us that it was morally neutral to inflict any cruelty on animals because they were, in fact, perfect machines whose seeming cries of distress were no more connected to feeling than, say, clocks that chimed on the hour. Thirteen years before Georgie first cycled to Aspen, the town was visited by another eccentric European who had migrated south rather than west, whose name was Albert Schweitzer, and who spoke of "reverence for life" — by which he meant *all* life. These two figures do not stand in isolation; they represent an expansion in consciousness — a granting to life more and more remote from our own of feelings we hold in common, and rights we claim as global citizens. It is this reverence for life in all its forms — lives we are shrugging into oblivion before we have even recognized them — that Georgie is demanding we wake up to. If we get through this political bottleneck that threatens all earthly species with annihilation, if our descendants have the luxury of looking back on our difficult passage, it may be cranks like Georgie — herself by then anonymous — who have nursed the seeds that permitted this globe, also eccentric, to reflower.

28.

Notes of A Half-Aspenite III

Like the Eskimo I have forty words for snow, though none of them are suitable for a family magazine. I manage to stick out the first two months of winter, but by early December it is time to make way for my masochistic renters. What Shaw said of the afterlife — Heaven for the weather, Hell for the company — is how I think of the indefensible split in my own life between Aspen and Phoenix. To keep some hellish company amid the sun and saguaros, I pack my Aspen journal, full of slanderous memories. Such as:

December 23, 1975
Katie Lee arrived in Aspen just in time to celebrate her birthday, and just before I was scheduled to replace the scurvy louse-grey carpeting that came with the house. Katie was a river rat whose dream in life was to blow Glen Canyon Dam; her party could double as a farewell to the carpet — select ingredients for a cake designed as a miniature Lake Powell, which Katie could literally blow. Su Lum and Barbara Lewis sculpted a chocolate box cake into a reservoir of runny chocolate pudding behind a wall of vanilla wafers. My first notion was to substitute a single small firecracker for candles and I consulted a friend whose sideline was recreational explosives. He assured me he had just the little number to do the job and no more, but as I brooded on walls that were *not* to be replaced, on guests' corneas, and on the host's liability, I decided to trust Katie's own destructive instincts.

Katie appeared in full plumage, draped in a floor-length gown she had sewn from riotously colored patches and that suggested a bedspread with cleavage. Wine and daiquiris were downed, Katie played the guitar and sang river songs, food was dispatched, and as guests croaked Happy Birthday the cake was deposited at her feet. With a cackle of joy she lifted her dress to reveal the essential Katie, kicked off her heels, shrieked, "Take *that,* Bureau of Reclamation!" and sent her right foot through the vanilla wafers. Chocolate ran like magma onto the doomed carpet. To cheers from the crowd Katie leapt into the middle of the cake, held her hem high, maintained a

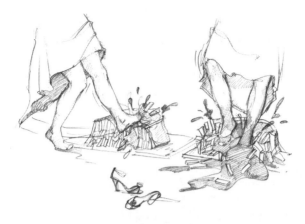

volley of Texan whoops, and danced like a peasant on vintage grapes. A viscous lagoon bloomed at her feet. This was clearly a cake that only the household ants would sample.

I emerged from my bedroom next morning to face what looked through my hangover like a dig at Pompeii. But what did it matter if the whole bottom layer was to be replaced? As I was soaping some glasses the phone rang. It was the carpet installers: the carpeting I ordered was temporarily out of stock, but they were sure they would have it in a matter of weeks . . . That was two months ago. Since Katie's departure I have been living with throw rugs angled irrationally over stains too large for them, as if feebly concealing a murder. Any future guest who wants to blow a dam will have to do it outside.

July 23, 1972

Got a dawn start over Independence Pass to Denver, rounded a blind curve, and suddenly six or seven kids on skateboards burst upon me like a flock of swallows. They swooped past before I had time to react. A glance in the mirror showed them either over the cliff or around the bend, and at least I didn't read about it afterward. May we all survive California.

July 19, 1978

The habits of a recycler die hard, and since there is no longer a newspaper collection I leave my *Rocky Mountain News* off at the Whale of a Wash. Had lunch with Kurt Oppens yesterday, and he mentioned doing the *Rocky Mountain News* crossword every day.

"I didn't know you got the Denver paper," I said.

"I don't," he replied a bit sheepishly, "but there's always one on the table at the Whale of a Wash."

July 30, 1986

I met a frazzled-looking friend on her way into a physics lecture at Paepcke Auditorium. "I don't know whether I can take this," she said. "I've just been to a dinner party where Mortimer Adler got into a raging argument with another guest. They went at it for an hour."

"Good heavens," I said, "what was it about?"

"The nature of Truth."

May 13, 1976

Learned that Kurt Bresnitz is a stamp collector when he caught me with foreign mail in my hand at the post office several years ago, and since then I have forked over any curious stamps when I've run into him at the post office. Just spotted his Wagoneer at the Recapture Lodge in Bluff, Utah, tore the stamps off a letter from Spain, clipped it to a note saying, "The Mad Philatelist Strikes Again," and secured it under his wiper. Another gift of the desert.

July 21, 1986

Guests wandering through a bonfire's corona, a sitar droning lightly to the thrum of bongos, voices agreeably muted, meatless casseroles being eaten from paper plates with chopsticks — it could have been a party from the late Sixties but for the pair of llamas on display in the corral and the chatter of workshops unvaryingly described as "intense." The woman I was talking with interrupted herself to ask if I'd noticed the locket on the young man behind me. "It seems to be a photograph of his *dog*. It's really refreshing. I can't see too well in this light, but I think it's a Pekingese. See if you can tell."

I turned and zeroed on the oval locket hanging from wooden beads, then tried to control myself long enough to say, "Betti, that's the Rajneesh."

June 12, 1981

On the first morning of a mule trip to some Baja cave paintings — that point when everyone exchanges backgrounds — one of my fellow travelers informed me that for many years he had been a florist in Glenwood Springs, owning what is now Niemann's Gardens. I had long been curious about that spectacular old glass building, and asked its origin. It had, I was told, originally been part of the Osgood Mansion in Redstone; the last surviving Osgood daughter still remembered breakfasting there as a child. I became excited: I had been drawn to greenhouses since early childhood, when it was my ambition to own one, and here was greenhouse history waiting to be researched. In the Sierra de la Giganta, riding the next mule, was the source of the next *Aspen Magazine* piece.

When I got home I dashed off two rhapsodic pages on the romance of greenhouses and how they pioneered modern steel and glass construction, then headed downvalley to interview the folks at Niemann's Gardens. To my horror only the central dome remained; the arms had just been replaced by graceless plastic arcs. The owners confirmed the Redstone connection, but said the old glass was extravagantly wasteful of energy and had to be replaced. They showed me where the thick bluish panes had been stored, and mentioned having been contacted by the current owners of the Osgood Mansion about the possibility of reconstructing the greenhouse in Redstone. Between the expense and the missing pieces they were skeptical. Meanwhile, despite prodding letters, I never received the promised reminiscences from the florist on the next mule, and the shards of the article, like the greenhouse itself, got filed away.

June 16, 1986

I saw my lunchmates were late, so ducked into a gallery next door, which turned out to be full of drawings by David Hockney. I viewed them with great pleasure, and told the owner so when he appeared several minutes later. He agreed it was a good show, looked at me oddly, and asked, "Are you David Hockney?"

"No," I said, startled, and gestured to the drawings.

"I have his work, but I've never met him. It would be typical of an artist to come in unannounced to see how the show is, and you look like pictures I've seen."

"Well, I'm not David Hockney," I said, and we proceeded to discuss the work while I thought on an inner track that I must have an all-purpose face, having been likened in time to Dmitri Shostakovich, a dancer named Russ Tamblyn, and a local singer. I saw my lunch friends approaching and started to leave.

"You could still *be* David Hockney," said the gallery owner.

"Yes," I agreed, "I could be lying."

October 17, 1982

A potential renter asked whether the transistor radio in the toilet paper rack actually worked.

"Yes," I said, "in fact it was there that I learned of the death of the Shah."

"From one throne to another," he murmured.

August 3, 1985

Music to soothe the savage beast. Because back problems have prevented me from sitting through concerts, I've taken to lying on the back benches during the loosely supervised Sunday morning rehearsals, figuring myself invisible once the scattered audience gets involved in the music. A friend just told me she can always tell where I am because the tips of my shoes stick up like the ears of an enchanted animal.

October 2, 1985

Left my lumbar roll at Ohl & De Vack. I dreaded having to account for the strange half-cylinder of corduroy that supported my lower back and to explain, if pressed, that it worked on the principle of the flying buttress, deflecting a downward force sideways. Asked the owner if an odd brown pillow had turned up, and he said, "That's the greatest pillow — where do you get them?" As I was describing the location of the therapy room at the hospital, the waitress came up and said, "Lumbar rolls are wonderful. I use one in my car whenever I have to drive more than ten miles." I half expect to see lumbar rolls on their next menu.

August 15, 1981

Got a call from Dino de Laurentiis, asking for a screenwriter who once sublet the house over Christmas from one of my renters. Wouldn't you know that when Hollywood finally called, it would be a wrong number.

November 19, 1985

Got some junk mail from the Citizens Committee for the Right to Keep and Bear Arms, promising me a Certificate of Merit if I would write my name on the enclosed form. I printed John Hinckley in block letters, mailed it to them in their postpaid envelope, and forgot about it. A month later, to my shock, there was an 8 × 11 envelope for John Hinckley at my address. Inside, in Gothic script and suitable for framing, was a certificate that read, "1985 Citizen of the Year awarded to John Hinckley affirmed by a unanimous vote of the National Board of Directors in recognition of outstanding individual effort in defense of the right to keep and bear arms."

July 15, 1979

Called my ex-renters to report I'd found their missing scuba gear, and got a recording that said, "We are currently not answering the phone to protest the holding of American hostages in Iran."

November 1, 1986

Went to an unusual Halloween party last night: we appeared as characters from *Macbeth* and did a reading of the play. Couldn't figure how to dress Scottish medieval on short notice, so I wrapped myself in a green bedspread, pinned olive twigs to my hat, carried a spruce bough and went as Birnam Wood. We read the first two acts around a bonfire, then went in for food just in time for the banquet scene in Act III. Ski pole duels, a papier-mâché head rolling downstairs and — best of all — the gloriously misread lines. My favorite:

> *Tomorrow and tomorrow and tomorrow*
> *Creeps in this pretty face from day to day...*

April 17, 1986

The furniture installed in the house when I moved in included a contoured plywood chair with four spindly legs, looking vaguely like an ice cream scoop on stilts. A variant of a model I'd seen here and there, it struck me as an ungainly bit of junk, but rather than pitch it I demoted it to the deck, where the sun bleached it from buff to ash and the surface sprouted asbestos-like body hairs. Years later a friend wandered onto the deck with a beer, froze, and said, "What are you doing to that *Eames chair?*"

"That what?"

He explained that Charles Eames was an American designer of the 1940s and '50s, one of our great originals, and that the chair was a classic. He had one himself that he kept in perfect condition. "Would you like this one?" I asked. "Perhaps you could restore it." After brief resistance he accepted, leaving me feeling partly stupid and partly relieved.

I've just come upon an article on chairs in the current *Smithsonian* by one Doug Stewart, who identifies the model as the "potato chip chair," and comments, "In 1950, the Eames shell was revolutionary. Today, it's just kitsch — something you squirm in while waiting for your laundry to dry." And I, in turn, will *stop* squirming.

July 19, 1987

Dropped into a gallery to see a retrospective show by an Aspen artist who had been prominent in New York in the Sixties, and found he was in the midst of an interview with the *Aspen Times*. "I notice that after the Sixties you switched from abstract expressionism to a more linear, hard-edged style," said the reporter. "Why was that?"

"Bursitis," came the reply.

July 11, 1987

Recently read an interview with a musician who said that the interruptions he most hated at concerts were the alarms on digital wristwatches. Yet at orchestra rehearsal this morning, while the conductor was explaining a phrase, that very sound erupted from the orchestra itself. A piccolo player, obviously with perfect pitch, came in right on the beat, joined next cycle by a flute at the top of its register and then, amid laughter, by what sounded like the entire wind section before the offender, invisible from where I sat, woke up and punched his button.

June 30, 1982

My piano teacher reported overhearing a lively argument between two patrons of the Music Festival over whether the upcoming Schumann Piano Quintet would be played on five pianos or by five pianists on one piano.

July 15, 1976

Was probably the only person at the Udall fundraiser who attended because of the Congressman's position on the House Postal Committee rather than his celebrated conservation work as Chairman of the House Interior Committee. Two years back I had received a letter from a friend in Holland who had printed IMPEACH NIXON on the envelope. The letter had been sliced open on top, clumsily resealed with Scotch Tape, and stamped, "Opened For Tariff Reasons." If there was a problem with the tariff — which I took to mean that it didn't have enough postage — it would seem more reasonable to weigh it rather than cut it open and, presumably, read it. Here was a clear example of our democratic government tampering with our mail, and here was someone in a position to look into it. After his brief, humorous speech on the prominent Starwood lawn, I went up to this ex-basketball player, craning my neck as if addressing a redwood, explained the circumstances and handed him the *objet.* "Opening mail wasn't at all uncommon during that period. Thanks," he said, folding it and stuffing it in his pocket so casually that I knew nothing would come of it, and that I had just lost my most treasured Watergate souvenir.

August 17, 1977

The chef salad at the Hyman Street Deli is of the uncuttest kind, a large wooden bowl of ham, lettuce and Swiss that requires extensive slicing and mixing on the part of the customer, while the only utensils offered are feeble plastic throwaway knives and forks. The frustration of all this labor made me attack the first bite so savagely that I broke off and swallowed half a tine — a mistake I didn't even notice until I started to spear the next bite. I took brief, queasy stock of my innards, then looked around the room for a reliable witness in case this event had legal consequences. At an outside table sat a local attorney sometimes referred to as the "hippie lawyer." I broke into his reading, displayed the remains of the fork and asked him to bear witness, which he did with only mild annoyance. Fortunately there were no consequences, legal or medical, and I vowed that next visit I would bring my camping utensils.

July 12, 1987

After a slide show on McSkimming Road broke up, Hillery and Luke found that their headlights weren't functioning and asked me to lead them the short distance to a house in town. We drove the four blocks carefully and without incident. I prepared to give them a farewell beep, glanced in the mirror, and saw flashing red and blue lights. I parked, walked back through a light rain, and explained to the officer that I was leading my friends slowly and cautiously home. He replied that it was illegal to drive at night without headlights, and he had to enforce the law. As the cop contacted the dispatcher and Hillery went through her car papers in the rain, a small man in a suit, somewhere in his late fifties, walked up and asked if the apartment they were in front of had an office; he was interested in renting. She looked up coolly. "No, there's no office, but the place has a sign. You could look the name up in the phone book and call."

"But I don't know where there's a phone."

"There's a public phone three blocks ahead on your left, at City Market," she said. We watched his figure, glimmering red and blue, make its way slowly across the street and on to City Market in the rain. "God," said Hillery, "if I have to deal with tourists even while I'm being arrested, it's time to leave."

October 23, 1969

We left the Chada Restaurant in Denver after gorging on Thai food, just in time to witness a car pull up to the fountain in the little triangle park across the street, five occupants jump out, run yelling around the fountain, jump in with their clothes on, splash each other, then pile back in and pull off, all in less than a minute. I didn't recognize anybody but I knew the style — a hunch confirmed when the car pulled off and I caught Aspen's own ZG plates.

December 11, 1986

Heading out on Highway 82, a Christmas tree slid out of the pickup ahead of me, missed putting its trunk through my windshield, and landed at the entrance to someone's driveway. Another Christmas miracle.

January 3, 1976

Was spending a family New Year's at my brother's in northern Michigan when a cry went up to ski. Don't worry, they assured me, you can rent equipment.

The clerk outfitted me with skis and boots, then said, "I'll have to see some identification." I pulled out my driver's license.

He peered and held it to the light. "You're from Aspen, Colorado, and you've come to Boyne Highlands to *ski?*"

"I go where it's at," I said, having seen the moment coming.

29.

Blood Country

It is late summer and the eye sickens rather than thrills at the first golden leaf. Or it is a late winter that threatens to devour the spring, and the eye glazes at whites and greys relieved only by the dull green of pine needles. Flesh is tired of trying to look presentable as a tourist, and itches for old flannel and jeans — or to throw off clothes altogether. Vision recoils from our tight valley and longs to rest its astigmatism on the horizon. Ears, ringing with traffic, voices and throbbing speakers, dream of space, distance, silence. The whole system calls for heat and hot color, and iron that reddens rock draws the senses like iron filings. There are remoter spots — Mazatlán, Bali, Katmandu — where Aspenites encounter the strange, the restorative and each other, but far more of them find a sense of release just by driving to Glenwood and turning left.

Southeast Utah is too seldom grasped from the bottom up, geologically. During the Mesozoic, roughly 240 to 63 million years ago, what is now Nevada and Utah lay in the shadow of the newly-risen Sierra Nevada Mountains. The basin was invaded by shallow seas, blown into dunes, and clogged with deposited runoff from the Sierras and the newer Rockies. Strata heaped themselves into layers that covered earth's mantle for thousands of feet. More recently — between 24 and 2 million years ago — the area was uplifted and cut into a vast and intricate canyon system by the Colorado River. Erosion, armed with seismic shift, blowing sand, and particularly with water, cut through the plateau, finding different fracture lines in each layer, and leaving freestanding spires, chasms, arches, caves, domes — an entire phantasmagoria that drought lays bare. More recent volcanic activity, pushing at the surface without erupting, raised isolated mountain ranges. At a median elevation of 4,000 feet, the slickrock country during the Holocene — today — tends to be idyllic in spring and fall.

One arrives from Aspen inevitably by car, stopping first somewhere on the plateau, where space reaches in all directions. The motor is stilled, and ears vibrate with what is either the after-whine or

157

pure silence, phrased perhaps by a single bird. Standing loosely around are pinyons and junipers, small aromatic conifers well-spaced so that none drinks its neighbor's water. The ground is a lumpy, crumbly, reddish clay. Here and there around the horizon, like arrested clouds, float the laccolithic mountains — the Henrys, the La Sals, the Abajos. A flock of pinyon jays may veer overhead, crying like wild oboes, or nothing at all may happen. Nothing: that is the open secret of this upper world, a nothingness into which one can heave a deep, liberating sigh.

The pinyon and juniper roof of this country varies little from place to place, whereas below the surface the landscape seldom repeats. The entire plateau is sluiced with canyons, side canyons and further subsidiary systems that challenge you to reach bottom. Some canyons are tiered through shales and soot-colored limestones that suggest a Victorian basement. Others soar hundreds of feet overhead in expanses of purest salmon trimmed with desert varnish, a streaking of blue-black minerals that leaks over the rim like the wings of crows. The narrowest of these canyons, capable of pinching to the width of a human being, may play the light back and forth down the naves of walls until the entire canyon melts in a sourceless radiance. Pale night-blooming flowers like the evening primrose and the jimson weed stay open all day. Footsteps report from pale sand, amplified. A seep in a canyon wall hollows an alcove hung with monkey flowers, maidenhair fern and tiny wild orchids, delicate as a Fabergé egg. Such canyons may lure you indefinitely over rock scrambles, around ledges and through clawed vegetation, or may stop you at a blackened shaft over a pool, to continue accessible only to birds, lizards and the imagination.

Methods of penetrating this country are various, including passenger cars, jeeps, boats and backpack paraphernalia. The trend over the years has been toward non-motorized travel, and those who really want to plunge in will lock the car, cram supplies into penitential backpacks, and spend a few days to a couple of weeks on foot. Here is the ideal solution: setting one's own pace, poking into any side canyon, scaling any wall that appeals, laying over for days in some treasured spot, returning to the car only when time and salami run out. The crucial requirement is water, and for this one needs to study contour maps, know the location of springs, the likelihood of potholes in a particular season, and how to keep out of the way when too much of a good thing arrives in the form of a flash flood.

While one definitively gets away from Aspen, one may not get away from Aspenites. At the trailhead one may spot Pitkin County license plates, particularly if one has kept up with the letters that have spawned from the patriarchal ZG. One reaches the confluence of Coyote Gulch preparing to greet strangers, and instead cries, Dottie! Murray! In one lonely canyon we were engulfed for days by thirty teens from the Colorado Rocky Mountain School, some of them raising their voices, and vowed we would consult their schedule before we planned another trip. And a friend and I backpacked Paria Canyon to wash the politics out of our systems after working for a Congressional candidate, and saw a storm gather behind us as we emerged. We became concerned for the redheaded Caudill family, somewhere behind us, where to be caught in rising waters in the six-mile narrows would be a serious matter. We reported their whereabouts to a BLM official in Kanab, who said they had already scouted the Paria drainage by helicopter and spotted seven redheads on a hillside, watching the waters rise.

Then there is Lake Powell. There is perhaps no way that water and rock, in conjunction, can be called ugly by anyone with an open mind, and Lake Powell may have more of that combination, in starker contrast, than any other inland body of water. Those without pride can extend the ski season on water skis, and by fall the lake is warm enough for skin contact. But Powell isn't actually a lake; it is a reservoir, and as such it is trimmed with oil slicks, bobbing styrofoam cups and the inevitable bathtub ring. It is, in fact, fresh territory for the internal combustion engine with its clamors and stinks. More unforgivably, it has drowned some 200 of the most idyllic miles of the Colorado River, along with its deepest side canyons, its sand bars, its cottonwoods and willows, its habitat for migrating herons and egrets, its tapestried walls that reached 2,000 feet overhead. Long, skinny and deep, Lake Powell can also be lethal, rocks like a tub in a storm, and has claimed the life of at least one Aspenite. There are those who return to Lake Powell year after year to fish the trout with which it has been efficiently stocked, but for those who love Utah slickrock, Lake Powell is a shroud, a vast winding sheet of water over what was the country's heart — utterly the reverse of what that country is about.

What that country is about, for Aspenites, is largely a longed-for simplicity. To a palate jaded by duck salad with raspberry sauce and linguine with pesto and goat cheese, it may be a menu that offers chile con carne with meat, potatoes au gratin with cheese, and pie à la mode with ice cream — or the special featuring three-bean salad and one-bean coffee — and that dreads the advent of yuppies with their spinach Florentine. Farther from civilization it is the astringency of juniper, the curries of mud and dust. To the touch it is the grit of sand, loose or compressed into stone, the grip of treads on pitched strata, the rake of brambles on clothing and skin, the shiver of air currents through the canyons. To the ear it is the clatter of wind through the cottonwoods, the single riveting of a woodpecker, the blown cries of pinyon jays, or bedrock silence that may be the beating of one's inner ear.

To the eye, the slickrock country is cleanliness, abstract design, and endless permutations of the color red. From red's thin band opens the spectrum of crimson, cinnamon, cayenne, rose, orange, rust, scarlet, maroon. Red sand has been pressed tight by old seas, hoisted into plateaus, fractured by rain, wind and ice, and pulverized back to sand. It flames from cliffs and mesas, bluffs, dunes and spires. Canyons open like the Red Sea, luring you in. Dispersed by the elements, it filters through the landscape, blows into food and cars and sleeping bags, is a denominator, a background radiation, the primary against which the other colors are measured, into which they resolve.

Southeast Utah's red is composed of iron, which occurs naturally in volcanic material and seeps into sedimentary layers. Highly oxidized iron produces the dominant family of reds, while iron that enters rock in an oxygen-reduced environment — undersea, in swamps, in decayed vegetable matter — produces a range of blues and greens we associate with coppers and cobalts. What brings all this chemistry home, quite literally, is that it is also iron, in the form of hemoglobin, that colors our own blood, and delivers life-giving oxygen throughout our bodily systems. Iron is the heaviest of our common metals, and the most complex element to be given off by the nuclear burning of steady stars. When we gaze out at a sweep of Utah slickrock, we are gazing deep into cosmic history, at the common origin we share with these rocks — all of us born in some previous generation of stars. The Utah canyon country not only gets into our blood; it *is* blood country, offering to claim us.

30.

The Ghost of Christmas Present

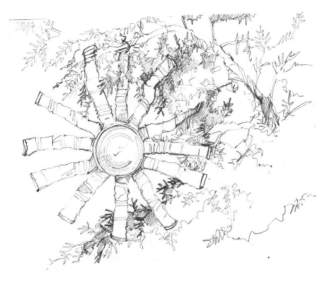

Hoarfrost clings to dried rabbitbrush and glistens on grass the color of straw. The sun tries to burn through milk, and December holds western Colorado in a subdued clarity: the edge of the desert and the edge of winter. Into this comfortable pallor, a mirage on the interstate median, springs a juniper wild with bloom. Can lids of every imaginable size, spray-painted yellow and blue and red, blaze from the tips of boughs. Cylinders of vegetable cans have been sheared into strips, then pulled from the lids into delicate stars. Some lids seem born to this task: pull-tops with their built-in hangers, paint can lids gleaming with pigment. The tops of ham cans contribute a teardrop effect. Lids without tabs have been punched with small holes and attached with twisties to individual branches and garlands of twine. The extravagance of decoration suggests long hours at the workbench, as well as unusual tolerance on the part of state troopers who frown on uncontracted landscaping. Like its cousin, the Mexican bottle tree, the wild Christmas tree thrives on desolation, turning its refuse into bloom. Plotted in secret, glimpsed at illegal speeds, unregistered by many of the eyes that process its color, the tree is a momentary catch in the vision, a Ghost of Christmas Present. Born to flash half-seen, eastbound and westbound it sends its bright constellation, a gift of strangers, anonymous as all desert miracles.

31.

Abigail and Pierre

It is too bad that beards have become as anonymous as sunglasses. A beard used to be some guarantee that its source was worth knowing, and I first saw Pierre's beard in 1957 while accompanying my brother-in-law across Aspen to collect the rent on a small cabin Pierre was leasing. Pierre must have been seated the whole time we were there, for my memory is of someone peering up with eyes of soft coal out of as full a black beard as I'd been close to, like a wild animal out of a thicket. The voice was warm, but to a teenager during the crewcut regimental Fifties Pierre was decidedly exotic, even threatening. I mentioned the strange person to my sister that evening at dinner, and she reassured me. "Oh that Pierre. Under it all he's so nice. . . . "

Pierre's name surfaced from time to time, once signed to a $10 donation during an impassioned Congressional campaign to rid our district of the earth-hating Wayne Aspinall, but I didn't encounter him again in person until fifteen years later, at a slide party for desert rats. Pierre, it seemed, was also a desert rat, was one of us, was perhaps even chief rat. The remembered eyes and beard were yoked by a flared nose, dark complexion, disheveled black hair and a bearlike frame supporting the comic drive of a Zorba. Pierre's laugh rang with the horizon as he poured us desert daiquiris: Wyler's lemonade and grain alcohol. Grizzled and expansive, Pierre epitomized the West — until he opened his mouth. His speech, irredeemably Brooklyn, was full of flattened *a*'s and the kind of inversion that turns *sawhorse* into *sorehoss*, inflections a Gotham linguist could accuse within six blocks. His beard, meanwhile had been salted by the years. . . .

Accompanying Pierre was a quiet and elfin lady named Abigail. Her own large dark eyes were set in a pale oval of delicate features, her hair tied in dark sprouts to either side, her soft voice explosive with laughter. Less assertive than Pierre, she revealed a quiet intensity and a comparable fanaticism about the desert. I first got to know her at parties where we showed off personal treasures: artifacts, campaign buttons, dolls, antique spoons, old postcards. Abigail's were always the most intricate and exquisite — beaded purses, jeweled buttons — and showing them her face would light up like some prize cameo from her own collection.

The fusion of Pierre's expansiveness and Abigail's containment exerted a minor fascination. One saw them every Saturday morning at garage sales, where they would pile from the car and swoop upon junk like magpies spotting a road kill. Their half-acre hideaway contains a shed three times as large as their house, heaped to the roof with boxes, cabinets and stacked oddments inventoried in their brains, if at all, where the minotaur might be a stereopticon or a stuffed duck. (A friend recalls finding a dish of broken keys and asking Pierre what it was. "That?" replied Pierre in surprise, "That's my dish of broken keys.") Most esoteric are sales of their own. I have seen perhaps a dozen customers at Abigail's row of double tables, utterly hushed, rapt in a feast of miniatures as if in a trance of hummingbird nests and dolls' negligees. Junk is clearly a bond in their relationship.

But there is another external which amounts almost to a trinity with the two of them, and it is the desert. For months they wander the wastes of southeast Utah, living out of a car that remains parked for days, keeping secret discoveries almost a blood pact between them, acknowledging some hideout they passed with no more than a shared glance even in the presence of close friends. But occasionally they broke seclusion, and their annual spring trips with a few intimates had generated a certain mystique, sustained by tradition and mutual farce. There was, for instance, a movie about one trip called *Six Came Back* (six, of course, left). I felt privileged to be let into their clique — and to spy on them at close range.

Most indelible was my first glimpse of Pierre eating lunch. With the air of an alchemist, his skin swarthy beneath a wide felt hat and the canyon burning from his mirror sunglasses, he pulled from his pack an array of Euclidian shapes which he proceeded to unravel. A gleaming tinfoil cylinder in ten equal sections, numbered from one to ten, dispensed the optimum portion of salami each day while doubling as a calendar. A smaller pocket offered banana leather, fruit which had been mashed to a paste, spread out to dry in the sun, then rolled fine and sliced to the dimensions of three consecutive Lifesavers. When I expressed admiration, Abigail said, "That's nothing. Pierre, unfurl the flag." Pierre drew a tube out of the pack and unwound a disk nearly a foot in diameter, an edible Joseph Albers composed of a circle of crimson on a larger circle of beige. He tore us each off a hunk, which exploded in our mouths into primal banana and quintessential strawberry. He rolled up the rest of the flag, then reached for dessert: three M&Ms and a lemon drop cradled in a miniature form-fitting ziploc bag. "Where do you *get* those bags?" I inquired.

"Make them myself on long winter evenings. One should ration one's junk food, don't you think?"

Abigail and Pierre's precision extends to the composition of their packs, in which every item knows its place and each article of clothing is folded and stored in a separate plastic bag. They are the most impeccable of backpackers. But if I thought their harmony was to be on permanent display, I was mistaken. I had expected our tight cabal to camp in proximity, gather around communal flames and socially blend. But when we reached our first campsite, Pierre and Abigail vanished over a hill until the next morning, while the rest of us further divided so that our party of seven was Balkanized into three separate groups. And so it has been ever since.

The seclusion is partly that the two of them — and Abigail in particular — detest campfires because of the smoke, the smell, the charred firepits, the elimination of dead wood, even the hypnosis of the flames, which for her is the camper's version of watching TV. Abigail, in fact, so dislikes evidence of human passage that she systematically erases their footprints before they abandon each

camp. But more fundamentally the canyons are for them an occasion for solitude, for letting place rather than company set the mood. As soon as they have picked their spot they pitch a tent, improvise furniture of logs or stone for their burner and implements: establish a retreat in which they are snug as mice in a teapot. Every campsite approximates a home from which they can go out to meet the world, then withdraw. Even their names for each other, Abigail and Pierre, have evolved through years of private reference. The apparent aloofness bothered me — until I caught myself imitating it. Here was clearly another kind of balance, struck between sharing and privacy, and an affirmation that communion can be the deeper for being discontinuous and voluntary.

By what route did two individuals reach such poise? Pierre began as the youngest of a large Italian family in Brooklyn. Throughout school he grew increasingly restless, wary of a set East Coast career, and he conceived the notion of finding himself in the wilderness. Already he was drifting from Catholicism, and his parents were sure he would wind up communist. When he mentioned the West, his friends conjured a waste of Indians and snakes where his brain would rot. Why not settle for the Catskills? After college, hovering between excitement and dread, he packed a design portfolio into his '46 Ford with improvised trailer, and aimed west. When he got to Ohio, all the voices of fear, guilt and recrimination came crashing in. Unable to continue, he got out of the car and bawled uncontrollably. Refreshed, he climbed back into the car fired with adventure embodied in the choice of roads splintering in every direction.

Pierre was struck by the friendliness of people who didn't seem to want anything. When a girl in an Indiana drugstore said, "Now hurry back," he took it for a proposition and replied, "Oh, may I?" He woke up under snow in the Ozarks with his beard frozen solid. He fished to save money, kept track of nickels and dimes in his diary. The world was newly invented. And somewhere out there, he imagined, was a dream girl, vaguely blonde and blue-eyed, who wanted to share all this. He reached Denver, loved it, found design work and holed up for the winter. In the spring he continued to Aspen, was hired as an assistant by a well-known architect, and continued working on assignments in Denver. His pilgrimage from Brooklyn ended in a three-room shack for which my brother-in-law gouged him $80 a month.

Abigail grew up in middle-class Denver. Restless like Pierre, as a child she read books on Himalayan treks and jungle expeditions, and envied boys their freedom. She dreamed of a man with dark hair, dark eyes, a beard and an artistic personality. After college she married a physicist. She already had reservations on the way to their honeymoon in California, when the groom remained in his suit and refused to loosen his tie across the Nevada desert because the trip was being paid for by the company, and the company had to be represented. They spent several years on the West Coast, then moved to Colorado Springs. Abigail watched the storms arrive over Pikes Peak, thinking that someone beyond there was doing something interesting and needed a companion to share it. Her husband, meanwhile, was planning to return to Denver, to a suburb Abigail particularly loathed. She foresaw a future of kids, broken appliances, small advancements, gibbering neighbors and boredom. She panicked, filed for divorce, and felt a great burst of freedom even as she went back to live with her parents. She dated a Denver architect who took her in the direction of the storms, to the 1963 Design Conference in Aspen.

As fate arranged it, Abigail's date was a Denver colleague of Pierre's. As soon as Pierre saw her he moved in, kept taking off with her, birddogged her, as they said in the Fifties. When she returned to Denver with her date, Pierre invited her to Mexico. Abigail by now was 34, but her parents objected that she hardly knew Pierre, and besides he was Italian. Pierre pelted her with postcards from Mexico, taunting her with what she was missing, and extended a standing invitation to visit him in Aspen. She began showing up for weekends, commuting, and gradually moved in. Not exactly blonde and blue-eyed, Abigail became Pierre's dream girl. Pierre became Abigail's dark and artistic stranger, though she hadn't counted on the appalling Brooklyn accent.

For Pierre, Aspen in the early Sixties was an extravaganza of celebrities, ski bums, cultured Europeans, ex-Nazis, saints and re-probates one could never encounter in New York. The town had utterly abolished social stratification; one lived in a single unraveling pageant. To Abigail the same types were rude, self-centered, egotisti-cal. Bored by the spiral of parties, she did not understand most of Pierre's friends, was in turn ignored by them, and found that many never bothered to learn her name. She adjusted to Aspen by staying on its edge and quietly designing dresses, many of them for the wife of the architect Pierre worked for. It was her greatest triumph that one of her gowns was worn to a ball in London and praised by Lord Snowden. Over the years Abigail has become more tolerant of Aspen, just as Pierre — like so many who lived through its later exploitation — is correspondingly disillusioned. What Aspen most gave them was the freedom to be obscure, to live tranquilly, and to remain unstructured enough for lengthy flights into the desert.

Like any decent harmony, theirs is a tension of opposites. Abigail is an early riser; as Pierre sourly notes, she gets up chirping. She spends the morning sipping the first five of her daily fifteen cups of tea, and gazing out the window. During the third cup she begins to cover one leaf of a small notebook with writing — thoughts, opinions, fantasies, plans. It is a form of meditation, says Abigail, and Pierre adds that it is dense as a brick wall. When she has finished, she crosses it all out and throws the page away. Pierre does not get to read it. The rest of the day, Abigail claims, is devoted to packing and unpacking, transporting objects from here to there. She is, says Pierre, utterly even-tempered, and a friend adds that Abigail has mastered the art of creative leisure.

Pierre, by contrast, is volatile and a night person. He wakes up late and dull, and thereafter suffers unpredictable ups and downs. I asked a camping friend whether he ever spoke to Pierre in the morning; after consideration the friend replied, "Only very carefully." His days are similarly unstructured, but come reluctantly to grips with the making of money. He supplements his meager intake with their garage sales and some wicked gin rummy playing on Saturday afternoon, though lately the regulars have been strangely dropping away. In a kind of symmetry, he experiences at night the solitude Abigail enjoys in the morning.

Pierre always felt that no one would put up with his moods, or deserved to, never presented himself otherwise or, for that matter, considered changing. He always thought himself too volatile to get married — and never has. Perhaps a large secret of his attunement with Abigail is that it is wholly voluntary, bright with open space. Abigail disappears for months to Denver to stay with her mother, with whom her relation is touched with the psychic, and Pierre spends part of every winter on the East Coast with his extended but close-knit family. Theirs is largely a case of compatible solos.

But it is so compatible that I pressed for details of any disharmony. Abigail, she admitted, grew up in the grim cheer of Protestant suburbia; resentments were suppressed, disagreements smothered, all hostilities conveyed with a smile. Pierre, as a second-generation Mediterranean, grew up fighting. Their only difficulties have occurred when Pierre has forced Abigail to look at something unpleasant in their lives, which Abigail admits is a painful necessity. Aware of her roots in suburban niceness, Abigail nonetheless affirms that she discusses while Pierre — raising his voice — argues. Pierre argues

167

that his voice is naturally louder. The content of those unpleasantries went unstated.

While Aspen was indeed that salvation beyond Pikes Peak where someone must be doing something interesting, it was never more than midwife to their relationship, and the cabin Pierre finally bought from my brother-in-law is increasingly overcome by the new, the noisy, the out-of-scale. But the desert is still radiant, and Abigail and Pierre have bought 50 acres of it surrounded by BLM land, outside a little town further west. Artifacts have turned up like bright omens. Abigail has found the perfect rock for sipping tea, sweet water spills from a spring and they plan, in a modest way, to build. They will rent out their cabin in Aspen, but hang onto it in case the social isolation drives them back. Aspen has that quality: its expatriates never quite let go.

Aspen, in fact, is a kind of turnstile through which a multitude passes slightly deflected from course. A few actually live there, but as a rite of passage it is a national institution. It is amply known for seducing dropouts, provoking divorce, swamping careers, peddling venery, narcosis, bankruptcy and base values. But occasionally it introduces an Abigail to a Pierre, nurses them until they are ready, then whirls them onward, bright but distinct, a binary star on some farther horizon.